Viola

The Magic of Music Theory

Primer

Kristin Campbell

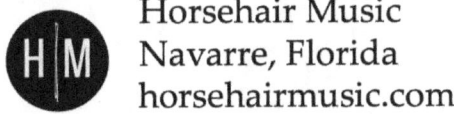

Horsehair Music
Navarre, Florida
horsehairmusic.com

All content in this workbook is copyright © 2024 by Kristin Campbell.
International copyright secured. This work cannot be reproduced in any form, print,
digital, or recorded without written permission from the copyright holder.

Primer Violin: ISBN 978-1-959514-12-1; Library of Congress Number: 2024914068
Primer Viola: ISBN 978-1-959514-13-8; Library of Congress Number: 2024914070
Primer Cello: ISBN 978-1-959514-14-5; Library of Congress Number: 2024914071

This book is dedicated to my mom and dad, Dr. Fred and Ruth Coleman who were the best practice partners I could have had. They sat through countless lessons, practice sessions, recitals and were my biggest cheerleaders. Without their sacrifice and commitment, I would not be the musician or teacher I am today. Thank you, Mom and Dad!

Thank you to my students who have tested these pages, found my mistakes and typos, and made these pages better. Thank you to my cousin and fellow Suzuki teacher, Ashley Poppe, who spent some late nights and lots of messaging helping me think through these pages. Thank you also to my mom who has helped craft sentences and edited each draft. Lastly, thanks to my husband, Matt, who has encouraged me and supported me when I was ready to give up on this big project.

Graphics:
Cover Design: Christiana Hudson and Kristin Campbell
Hand image by www.vectorportal.com
Violin, viola, cello, bass, fingerboard, bow, baroque bow and coloring pages are copyright © 2024 Kristin Campbell.
All other images are in the public domain from www.freesvg.com
Aural Skills recordings: Kristin Campbell

To the student:

Welcome to the Magic of Music Theory! Did you know that when you write things on paper it helps you remember them? This book is to help you remember things that you have learned in your lesson about your viola. This book will help you learn how to read and write music. Your practice partner will help you to read and do each lesson. If you have any questions, be sure to ask your teacher. When you finish this book, you will know and understand more about your viola and playing music. It's like magic, the magic of music theory!

To the practice partner:

You are the viola hero. Practicing isn't always fun, and it's not always easy. But in this journey of learning to play the viola, you get to walk alongside a child and give them the gift of music that will last for a lifetime.

My hope with this series is that it creates happy memories as you work through the book together. Playing games, reading stories, coloring, listening to music, learning how to draw and write music. Depending on age and reading ability, you may need to read the pages to the student. You can learn along with them. Don't be afraid to help and lead the student to the answer. These might new concepts and your child may not grasp it the first time it is introduced. That's ok! You will find a lot of review built in through out the book and they will begin to understand and remember. This is the process of learning.

Keep theory time short! You can choose to do the lesson at the end of one practice session, or you could choose to divide it up with just a little bit each day. It's up to you. Ask your teacher if they would like to do the "What Do You Hear?" pages in the lesson or if you should do them at home. You can access videos online or download free mp3 tracks with each question played on a viola. The answers for each question are given on the video/ track, so that the student gets immediate feedback in the learning process. I hope you enjoy the magic of learning music theory.

To the teacher:

I created this series because I realized that my students needed some basic skills before starting note reading. I needed something they could do at home, so I wasn't giving up valuable lesson time. By writing and drawing, I wanted to engage a different part of their thinking in the music learning process. This series teaches students recognize, draw music notation, symbols, reading notes on the staff and relates it to the fingerboard. The aural skills pages, "What Do You Hear?" can be done in the lesson, through online videos or using free mp3 tracks. The QR code will take you to the online video. To download the mp3 tracks visit horsehairmusic.com. Suggested recordings are linked to online videos to listen to while doing the coloring pages, but feel free to select your favorite artist or recording to share with your student.

You can also find the games and flashcards as a pdf download at horsehairmusic.com. This allows you to download and print the games in color or print the flashcards on heavier cardstock.

4

Table of Contents

Lesson 1

There are 4 different instruments in the **string family**: the violin, viola, cello, and bass.

The **violin** is the smallest member of the string family and plays the highest notes. People who play the violin are called violinists.

The **viola** [vee-oh-la] is a little bigger than the violin and can play 5 notes lower than the violin. The player rests the instrument on their shoulder for both the violin and viola. People who play the viola, are called violists [vee-oh-lists].

The **cello** [chel-lo] plays lower notes than the violin or viola. A person who plays the cello is called a cellist [chell-ist]. The cellist sits down to play. A long metal stick, called an endpin, rests on the floor allowing the cello to rest between the player's knees.

The **double bass** is the largest member of the string family and plays the lowest notes. Sometimes we call it "bass" for short. We pronounce this word "base," like baseball, not "bass" like the fish. The player stands or sits on a tall stool to play. People who play the bass are called bassists [base-ists].

The string family spends a lot of time playing together. It is important that we get to know and understand the other instruments in our string family. When a group is made up of only stringed instruments, it is called a **string orchestra**. When the string family plays with brass instruments (trumpets, trombones, French horns, tubas), woodwind instruments (flutes, oboes, clarinets, bassoons), and percussion instruments (drums, triangle, xylophones, cymbals, piano) it is called a **symphony** [sim-phone-ee] **orchestra.**

Here are the parts of the viola and the bow.

1. Point to each one and say its name.

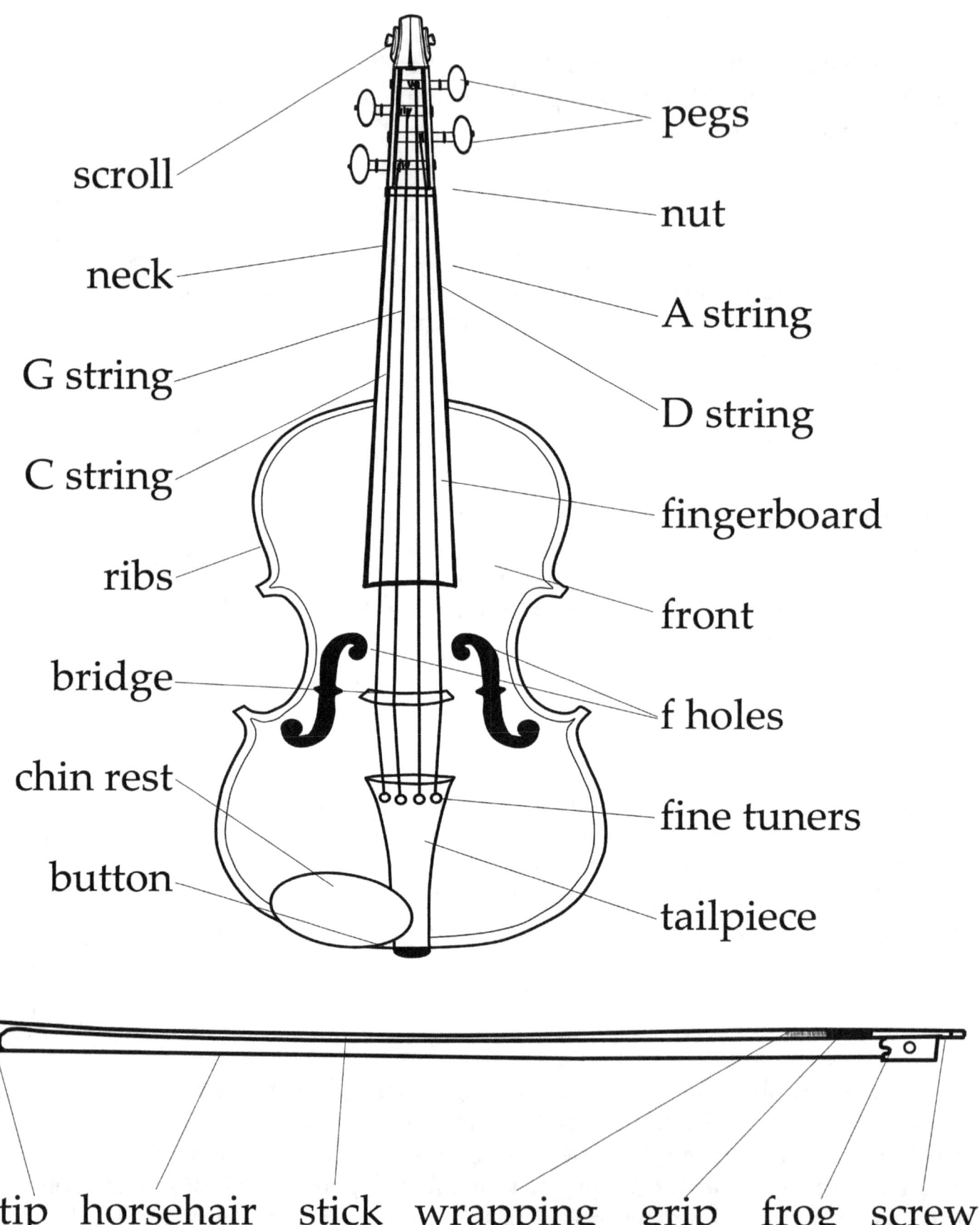

scroll

pegs

nut

neck

A string

G string

D string

C string

fingerboard

ribs

front

bridge

f holes

chin rest

fine tuners

button

tailpiece

tip   horsehair   stick   wrapping   grip   frog   screw

2. Draw a line from the term to the correct part on the viola and the bow.

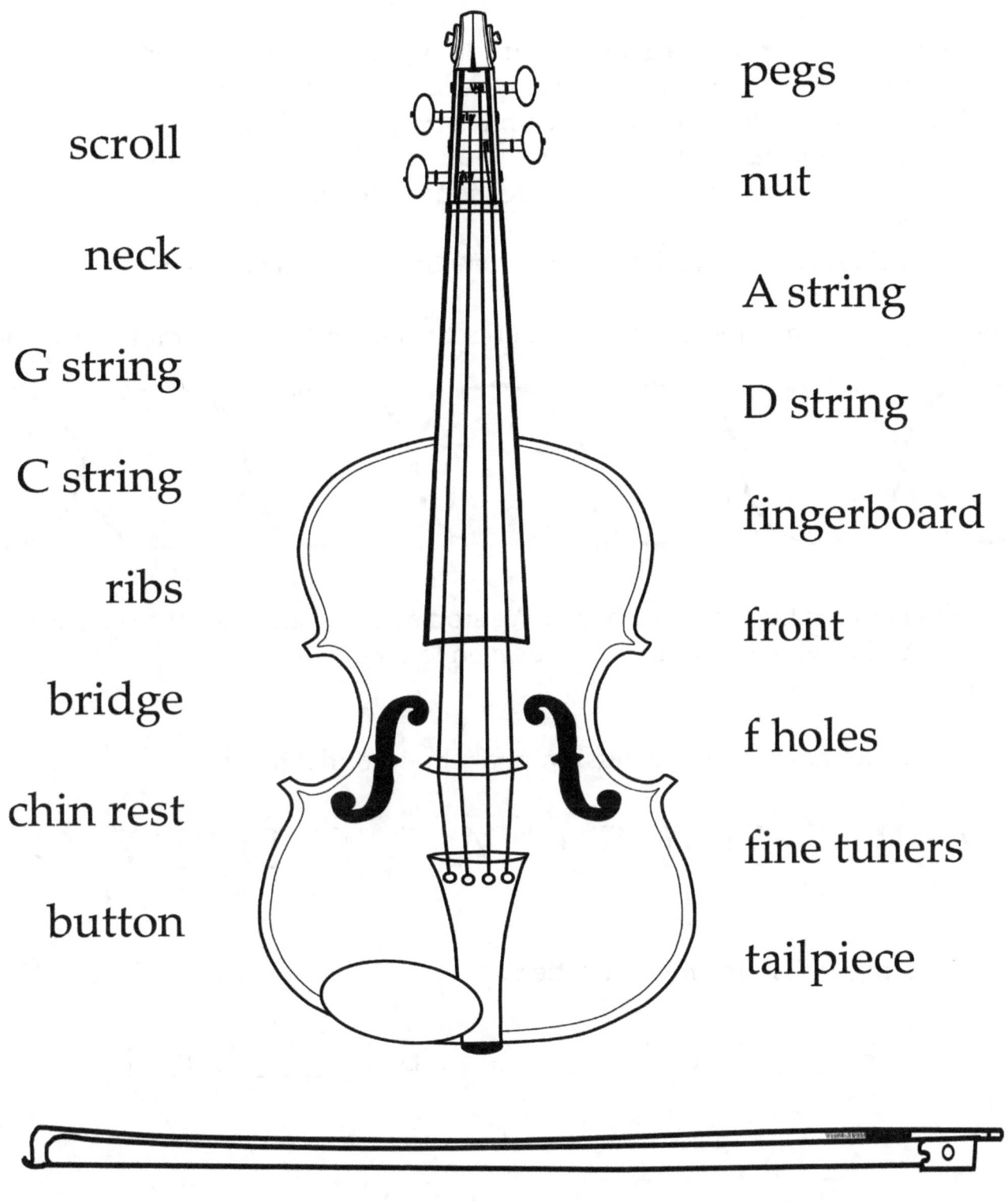

scroll

neck

G string

C string

ribs

bridge

chin rest

button

pegs

nut

A string

D string

fingerboard

front

f holes

fine tuners

tailpiece

stick   frog   grip   wrapping   frog   horsehair   tip

Lesson 2

What makes music? There are four elements that make music.

1. **Pitch** is the sound of each note. A group of pitches makes a **melody**. Pitches can move up, down, or stay the same in a melody.
2. **Rhythm** is how long or short each pitch in the melody is held.
3. **Dynamics** means volume. It is how loud or soft to play the notes.
4. **Harmony** is when two or more notes sounds together.

To identify pitches, we use the first seven letters of the English alphabet.

1. Write the first seven letters of the alphabet in the circles to see the music alphabet.

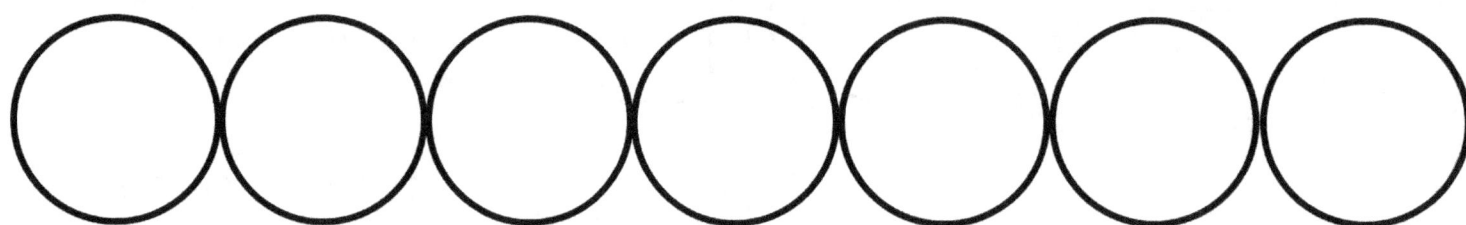

There is NO H in the the music alphabet! We stop at G. When you get to G, start over at the letter A. We keep repeating the first seven letters.

2. Point to each letter and say the music alphabet out loud 2 times.

A B C D E F G A B C D E F G

3. Who is missing? Fill in the missing letters.

A ____ C D E ____ G A B C ____ E F G

A B ____ D E F ____ A B C D ____ F G

____ B C ____ E F G A ____ C D E F ____

A B C ____ E ____ G ____ B C D ____ F ____

Fingerboard Power!

Each string on a stringed instrument sounds a pitch which has a letter name. When we play these strings with no fingers on the string, they are called **open strings**. Look at the open strings for each instrument in the string family.

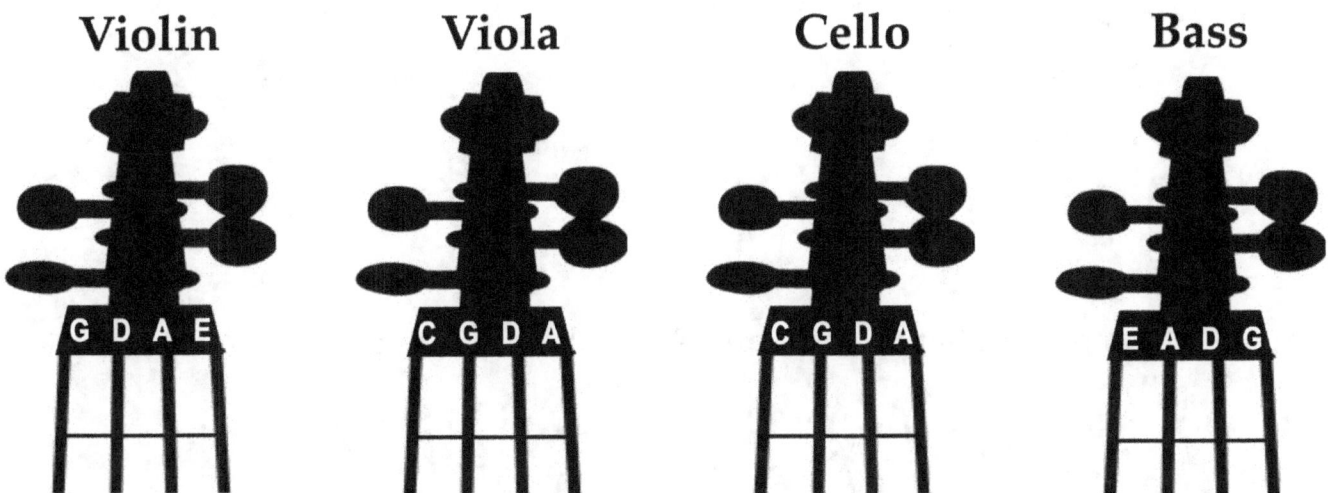

Violin **Viola** **Cello** **Bass**

G D A E   C G D A   C G D A   E A D G

4. There are three open strings that are the same letter on each instrument. What are the open string letters that all stringed instruments have in common?

_____ _____ _____

5. Draw a line from the term to the correct part of the viola.

chin rest

scroll

G string

C string

neck

ribs

bridge

fine tuners

button

D string

pegs

nut

A string

fingerboard

front

f holes

tailpiece

Lesson 3

To play the viola, the left hand holds the viola, and the right hand holds the bow.

Left Hand   **Right Hand**

1. Write an "L" on the left hand. Write an "R" on the right hand.

Each finger on the left hand has a number. The circle beside each horizontal line on the fingerboard shows where each finger is placed on the fingerboard.

2. Draw a line matching the finger number to the number in the circle.

 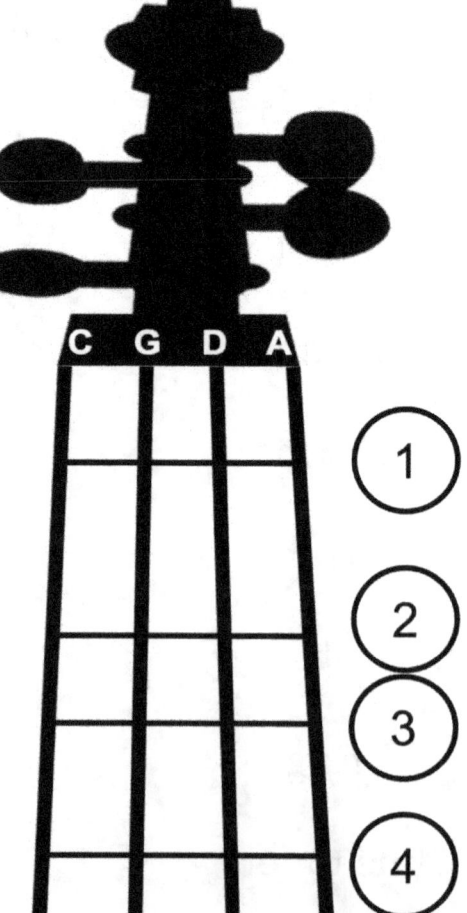

3. Write the finger number in each circle by the fingerboard. Write the correct finger number on each finger. Draw a line from the finger to the matching finger number by the fingerboard.

4. Color the left hands green and the right hands purple.

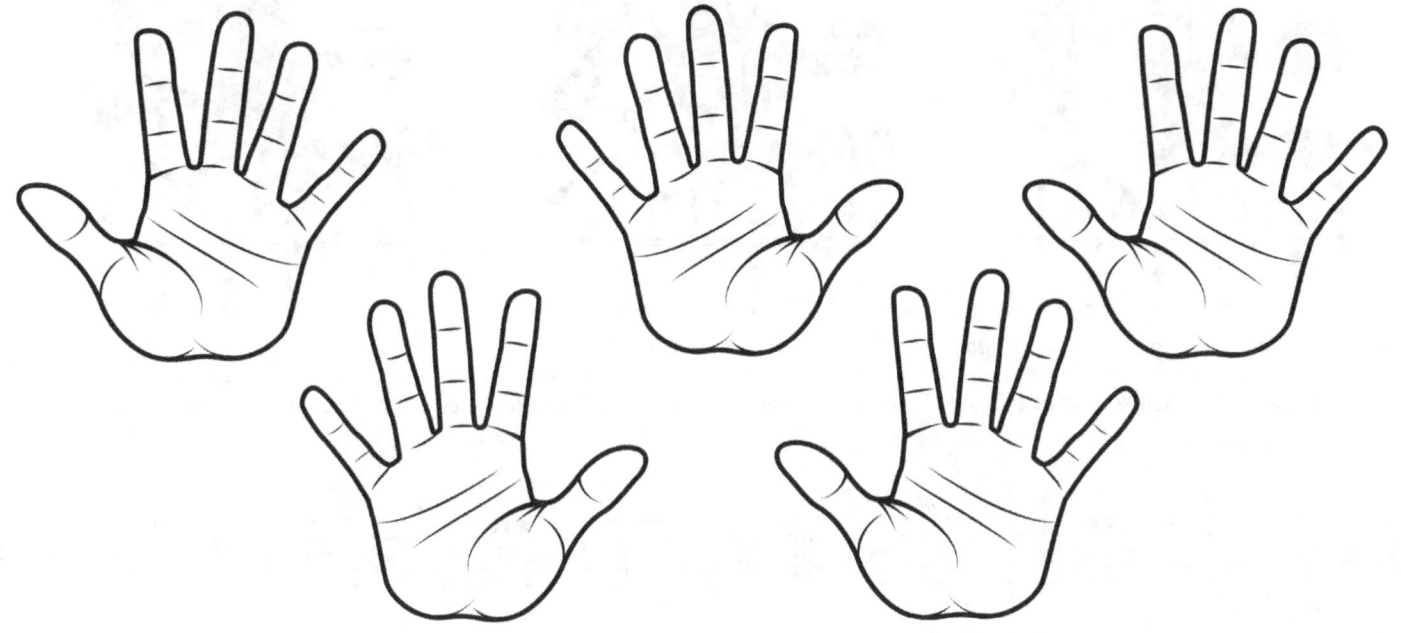

What do you hear? #1

You will hear 3 notes. If the notes you hear are high, color the bird. If the notes you hear are low, color the worm.

1.

2.

3.

You will hear 3 notes. If the notes you hear are loud, color the boy yelling. If the notes you hear are soft, color the girl reading.

4.

5.

6.

You will hear a rhythm pattern on an open string. Color the house of the open string that you hear.

7.

8.

9.

Additional ear training exercises can be found on p. 92 & 93..

Choose from these examples. For questions 4 – 6, add a dynamic *f* or *p*. For questions 7 -9, choose a rhythm pattern to play on an open string.

14

Pegs

Tailpiece

Front

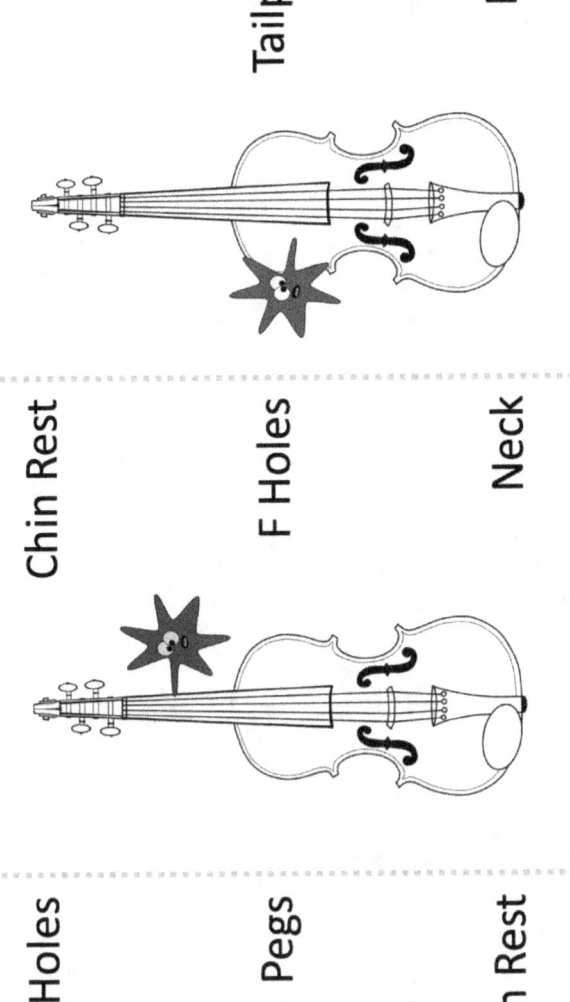

Chin Rest

F Holes

Neck

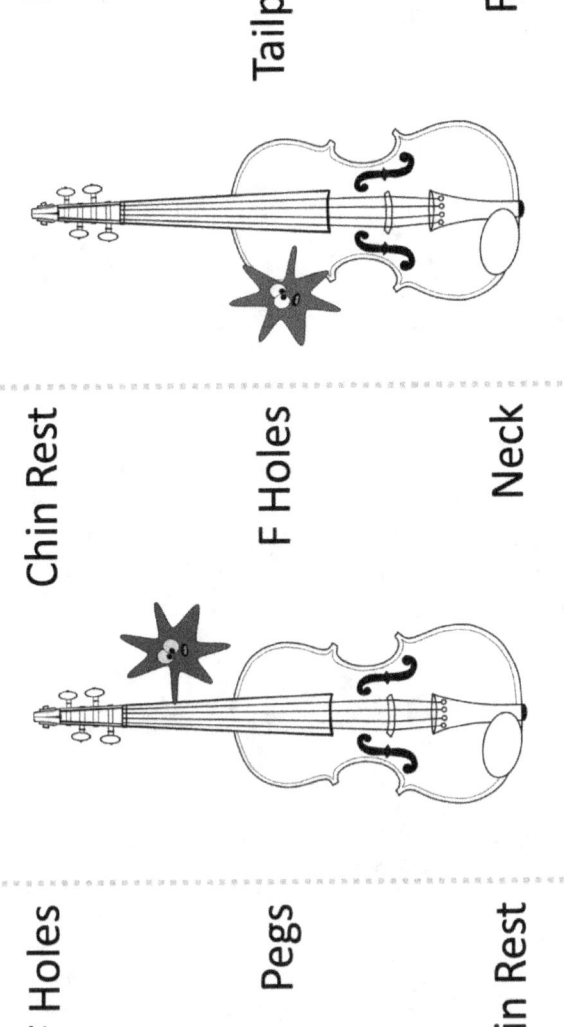

F Holes

Pegs

Chin Rest

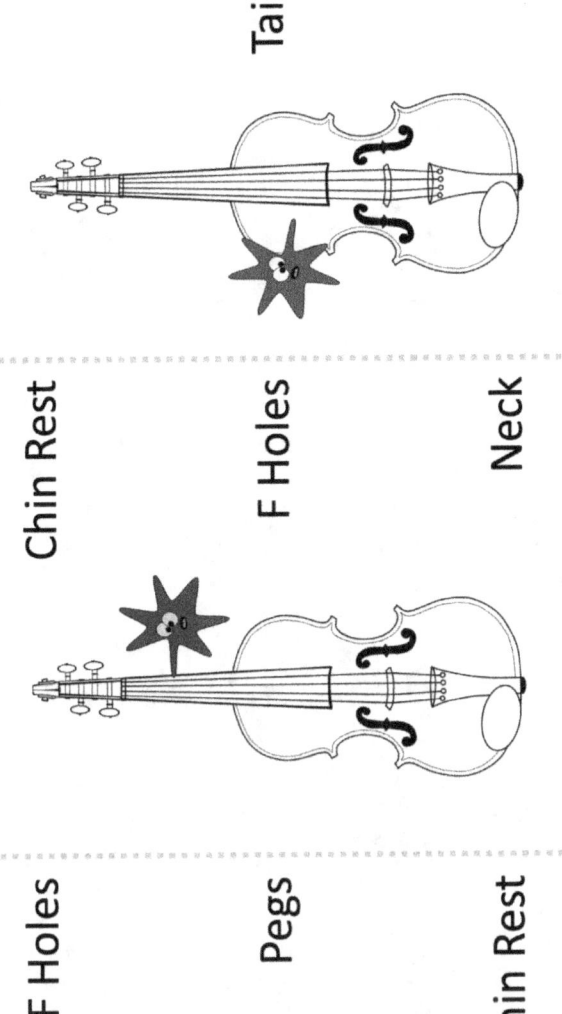

Fingerboard

Tailpiece

Strings

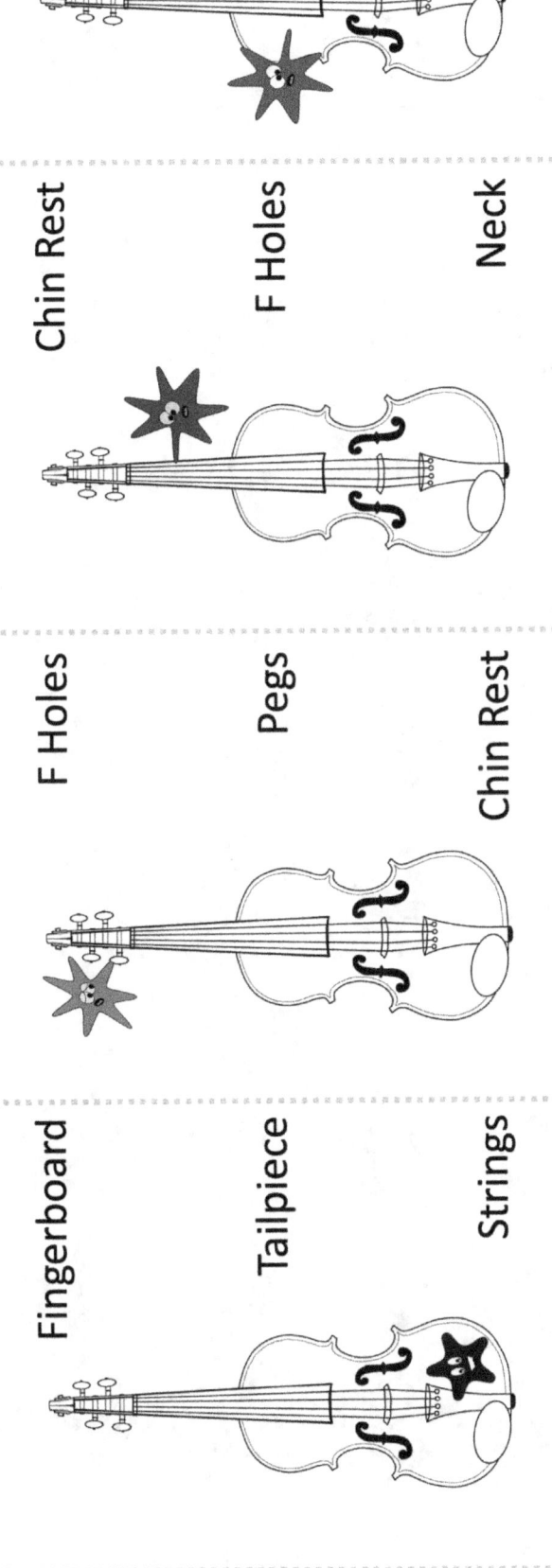

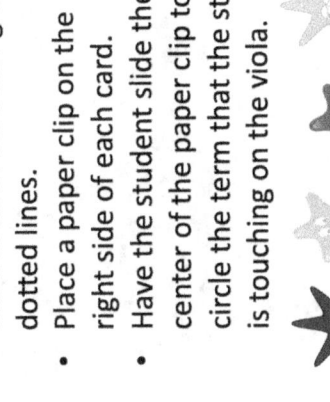

Parts of the Viola Clip Cards

- Cut out each card along the dotted lines.
- Place a paper clip on the right side of each card.
- Have the student slide the center of the paper clip to circle the term that the star is touching on the viola.

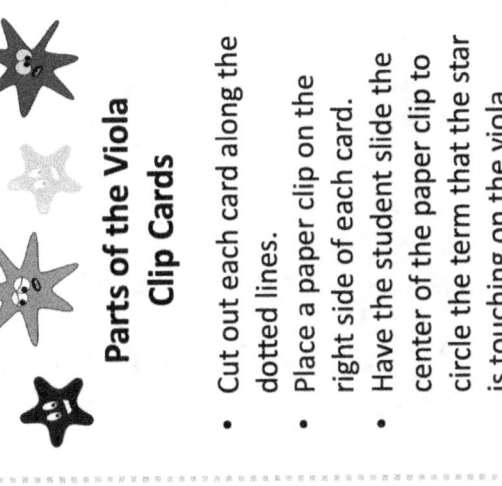

Scroll

Ribs

Pegs

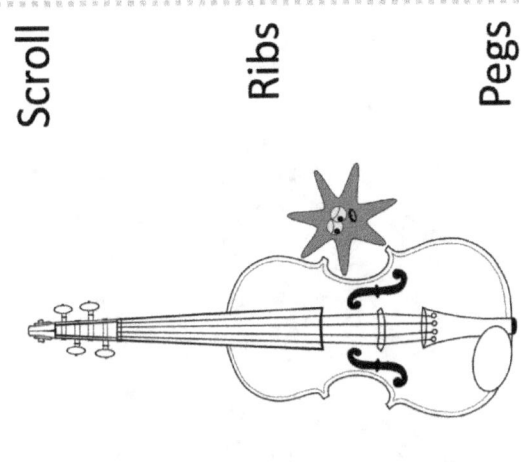

Fine Tuners

Scroll

Nut

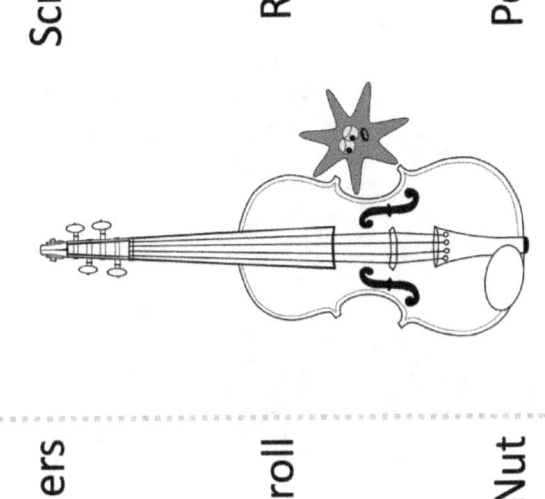

Bridge

Pegs

Chin Rest

© 2024 Horsehair Music

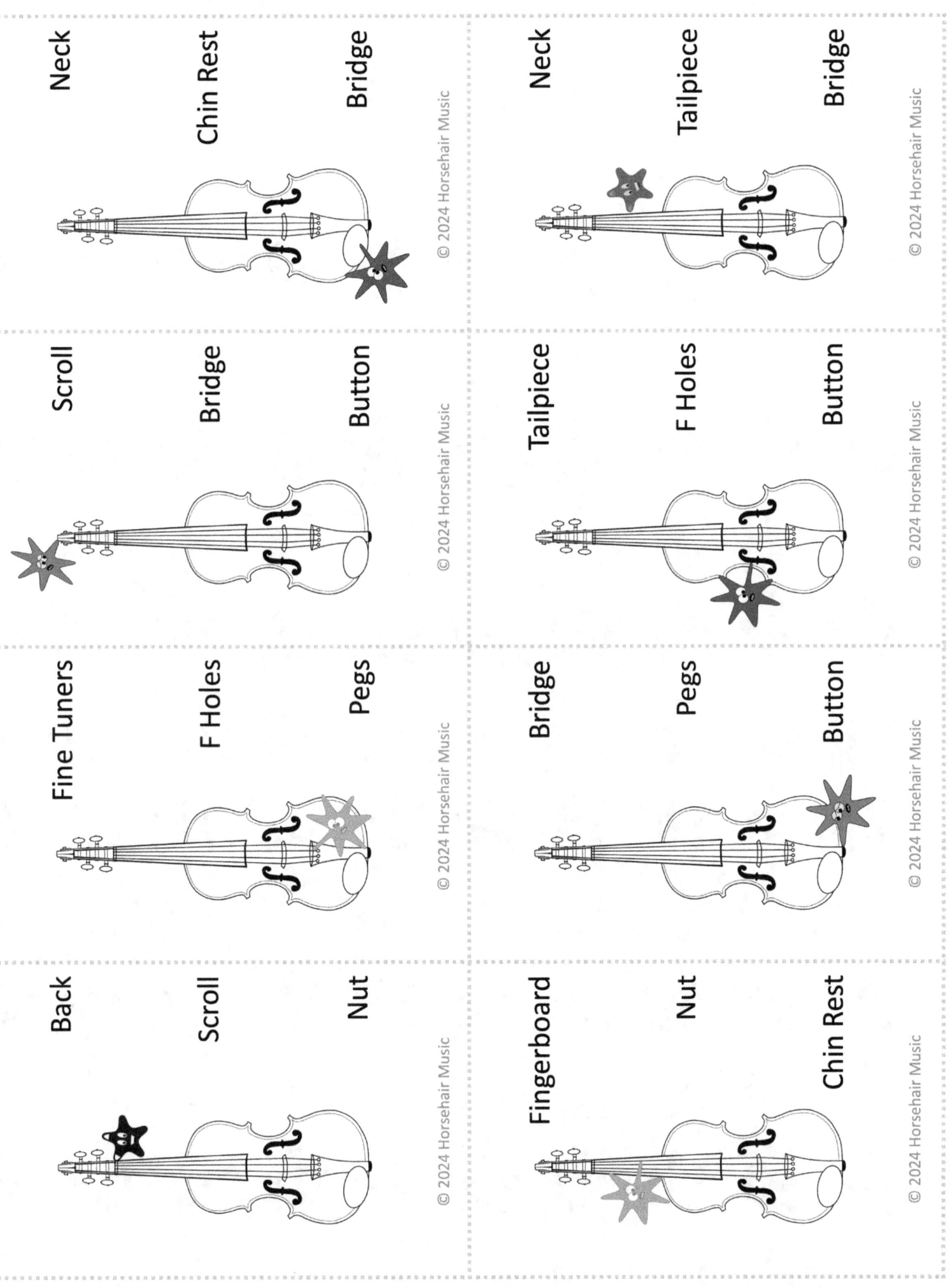

Neck — Chin Rest — Bridge

Neck — Tailpiece — Bridge

Scroll — Bridge — Button

Tailpiece — F Holes — Button

Fine Tuners — F Holes — Pegs

Bridge — Pegs — Button

Back — Scroll — Nut

Fingerboard — Nut — Chin Rest

© 2024 Horsehair Music

Lesson 4

Rhythm is how long or short we hold a pitch. Music notes show the player how long or short to hold a note. Each part of the note has a name. The round part is the **note head**. The **stem** is the straight line. Rhythm is measured in beats. Just like your body has a beat, a heartbeat, music also has a beat. Different notes show us how long or short to hold each note. Each note is held a specific number of beats.

This is a **quarter note**.
A quarter note gets
1 beat.

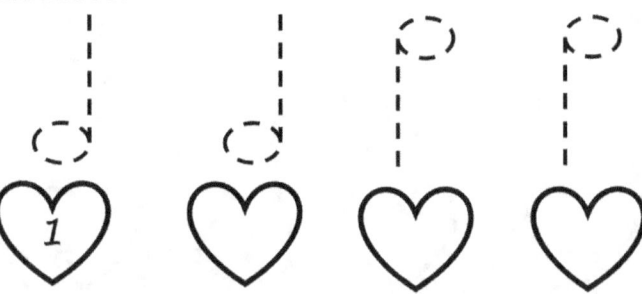

1. Trace the dots. Color in each note head to make it a quarter note. Write a 1 in the heart under each quarter note.

2. Clap each note and say its name, "quarter." beat, "1."

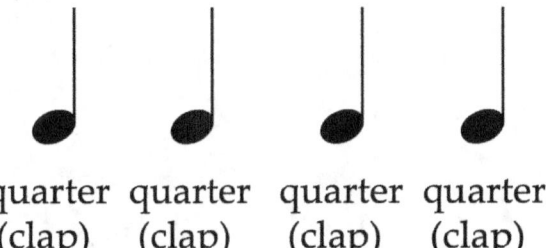

quarter   quarter   quarter   quarter
(clap)   (clap)   (clap)   (clap)

3. Clap on each note and say its beat, "1."

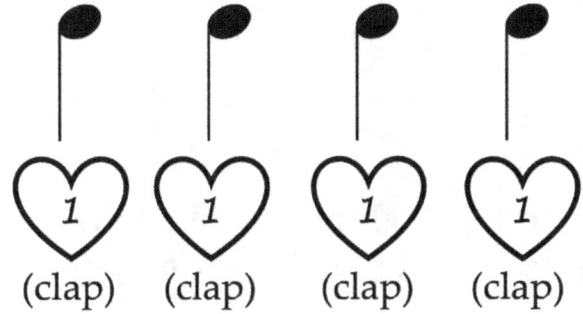

(clap)   (clap)   (clap)   (clap)

How to draw a quarter note:

Step 1: Draw a circle.   ○

Step 2: Color the circle.

Step 3: Draw a stem going up on the right side of the note head or down on the left side of the note head.

"stems go up on the right" or *"down on the left"*

19

4. Draw one quarter note in each box. Draw a circle and color it in. Add a stem going up on the right or down on the left.

Up Stem	Up Stem	Down Stem	Down Stem

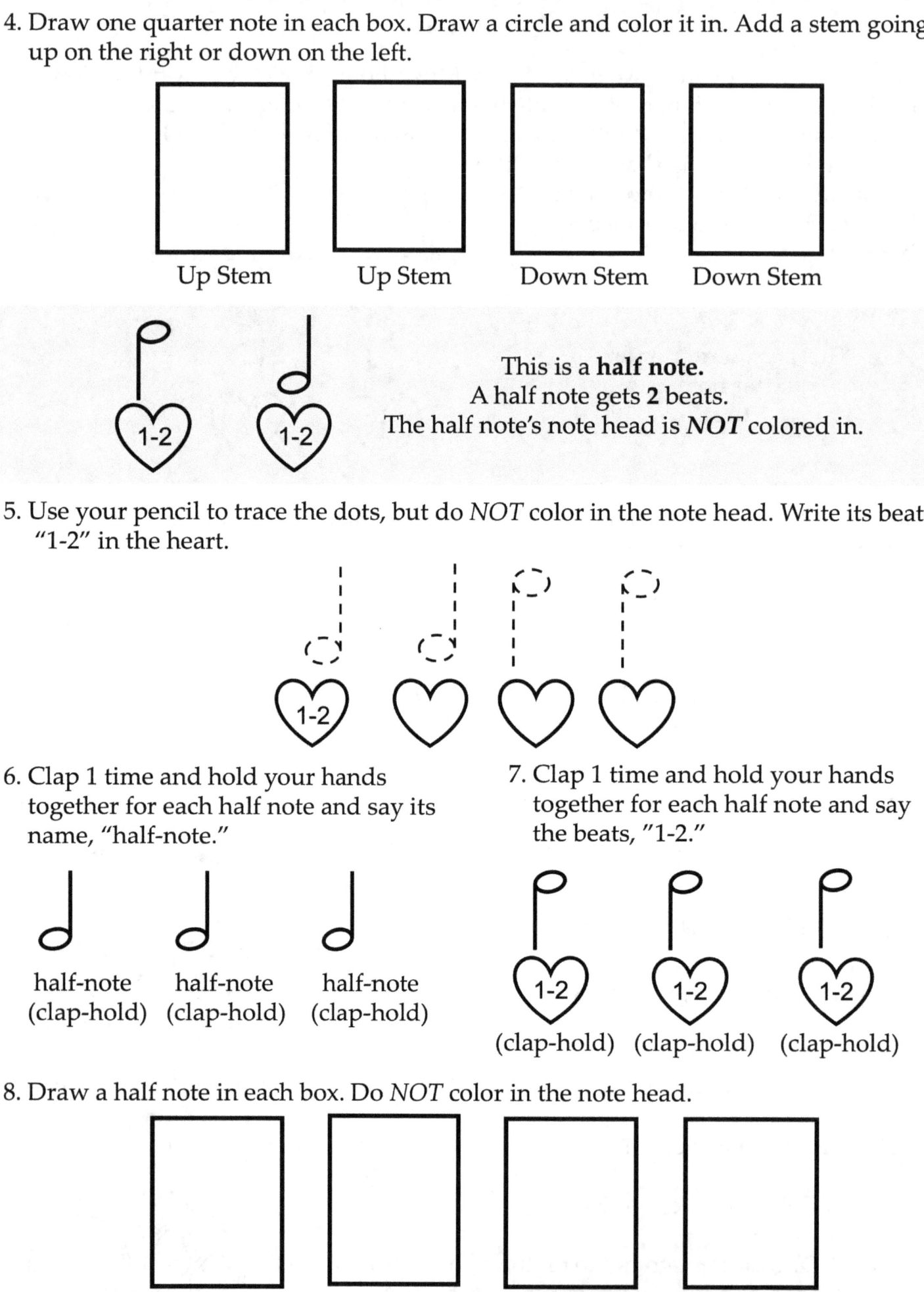

This is a **half note.**
A half note gets **2** beats.
The half note's note head is **NOT** colored in.

5. Use your pencil to trace the dots, but do *NOT* color in the note head. Write its beats "1-2" in the heart.

6. Clap 1 time and hold your hands together for each half note and say its name, "half-note."

half-note half-note half-note
(clap-hold) (clap-hold) (clap-hold)

7. Clap 1 time and hold your hands together for each half note and say the beats, "1-2."

1-2 1-2 1-2
(clap-hold) (clap-hold) (clap-hold)

8. Draw a half note in each box. Do *NOT* color in the note head.

Up Stem	Up Stem	Down Stem	Down Stem

Lesson 5

Dynamics means volume. We use Italian words to show what dynamic to play. **Forte** [for-tay] means loud. **Piano** [pee-an-oh] means soft. Only the first letter of each word written in a fancy script is used to show the dynamic.

f = *forte* = loud p = *piano* = soft

Circle the dynamic that describes the picture, f for loud or p for soft.

1. f or p	2. f or p
3. f or p	4. f or p
5. f or p	6. f or p

7. What is an activity you do that is *forte?* _____

8. What is an activity you do that is *piano?* _____

21

9. Draw a line from the term to the correct part of the bow.

stick   horsehair   frog   wrapping   screw   grip   tip

10. Write one letter of the music alphabet in each train car. Then read the music alphabet out loud 1 time.

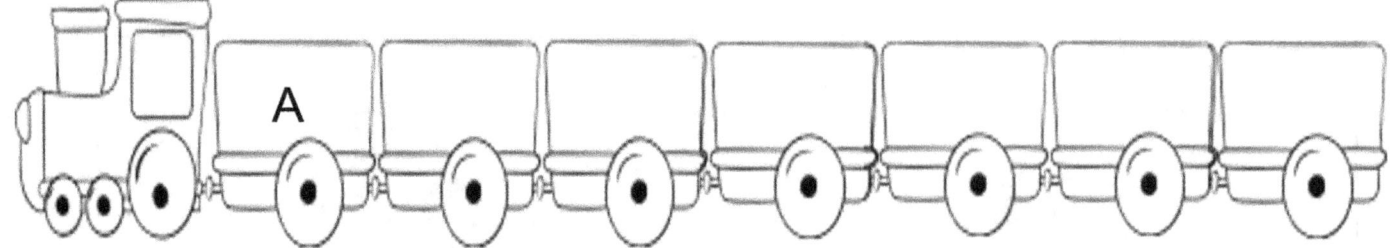

A

11. Write one letter in each train car of the music alphabet *going backwards*. Then, read it out loud 3 times.

G

12. Draw a circle around the notes with correct stems. Draw an X through the notes with incorrect stems.

13. The music alphabet can begin on any letter in the music alphabet. Read out loud the following music alphabets that go up beginning on a letter other than A.

C D E F G A B C D E F G A B C

F G A B C D E F G A B C D E F

14. Write the music alphabet going up beginning on E.

22   ___ ___ ___ ___ ___ ___ ___ ___

Lesson 6

1. Write the number of beats for each note in the heart.

2. Write the number of beats for each note in the hearts, then add them together.

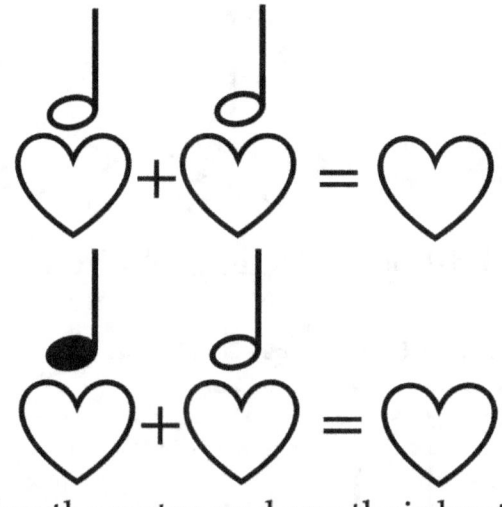

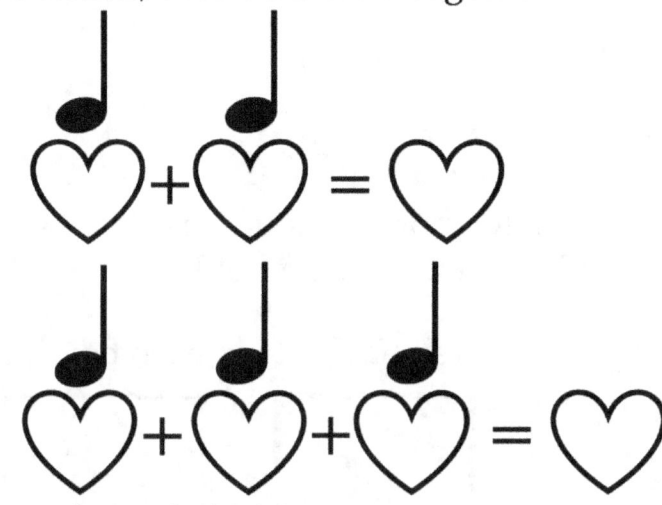

3. Clap the notes and say their beats. Then clap and say their names.

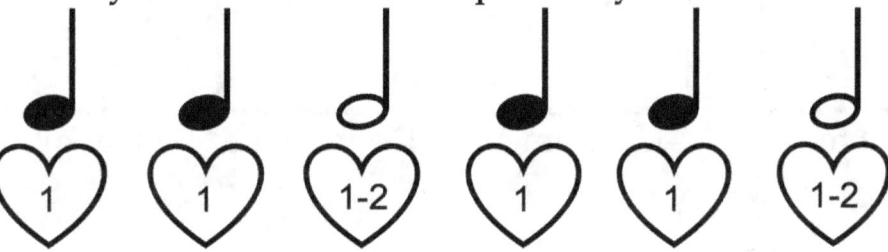

4. Draw the note that matches the number of beats.   5. Fill in the blanks.

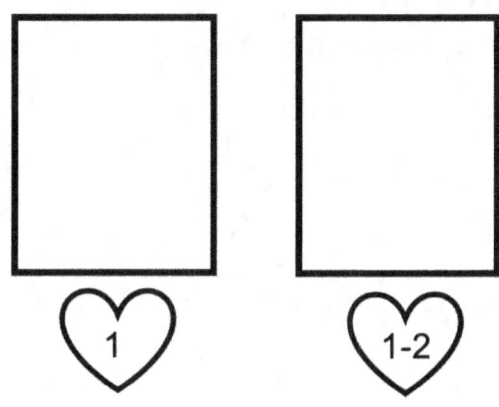

Stems go _____ on the right,

or _____ on the left.

This is a **dotted half note**. It is a half note followed by a dot. It gets 3 beats. The dot ALWAYS goes on the right side of the note head.

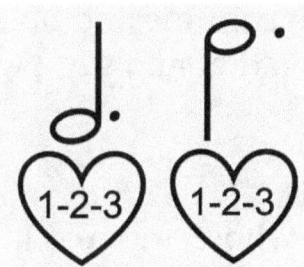

23

6. Trace the dotted half notes. Write the beats in the hearts.

 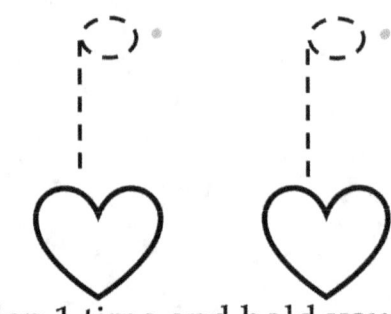

7. Clap 1 time and hold your hands together and say "half-note-dot."

8. Clap 1 time and hold your hands together and say the beats, "1-2-3."

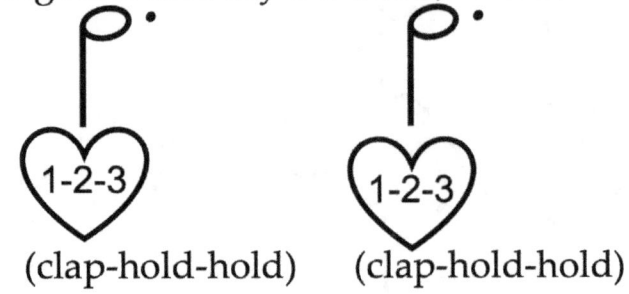

half - note - dot   half - note - dot
(clap-hold-hold)   (clap-hold-hold)

(clap-hold-hold)   (clap-hold-hold)

9. Draw a dotted half note in each box. Remember, the dot is ALWAYS on the right.

Up Stem	Up Stem	Down Stem	Down Stem

This is a **whole note.**
A whole note gets 4 beats.
A whole note does not have a stem.

10. Trace the whole notes and write the beats in the blank under each note.

11. Clap 1 time and hold your hands together and say, "whole-note-4-beats."

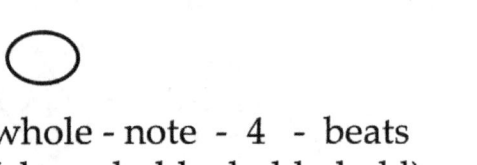

whole - note - 4 - beats
(clap - hold - hold - hold)

12. Clap 1 time and hold your hands together and say the beats, "1-2-3-4"

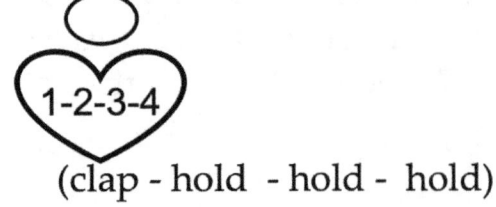

(clap - hold - hold - hold)

What do you hear? #2

You will hear several notes for each box. When you hear a long note, draw a line. When you hear a short note, draw a dot. Draw all the notes that you hear, in the order that you hear them.

Long Note = ━━━━ **Short Note =** •

1.

2.

3.

4.

* *Additional ear training exercises can be found on p. 94.*

Choose from these examples.

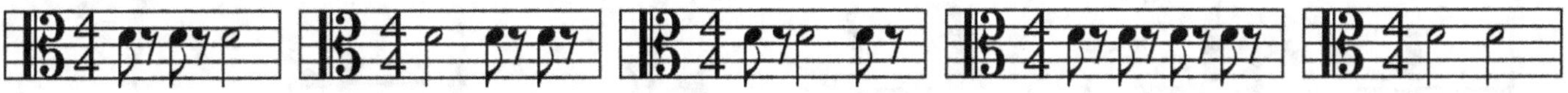

Lesson 7

In music, the speed of the music is called the **tempo.** Like dynamics, Italian words are used for tempo markings.

Adagio [a-da-shgee-oh] – slow
Andante [ahn-don-teh] – a walking pace
Allegro [a-leg-row] – fast, happy with energy

1. Draw a line from the term to the animal that matches the tempo mark.

Adagio   **Andante**   **Allegro**

Fingerboard Power! Each place we set our fingers on the D string is a pitch and has a letter name. As we set fingers onto the fingerboard, we go forward through the music alphabet. The letter "F" has a ♯ by it. This is called a **sharp**. Second finger on the D string plays "F-sharp."

2. Write the D string letters in each house and the finger number in the circle.

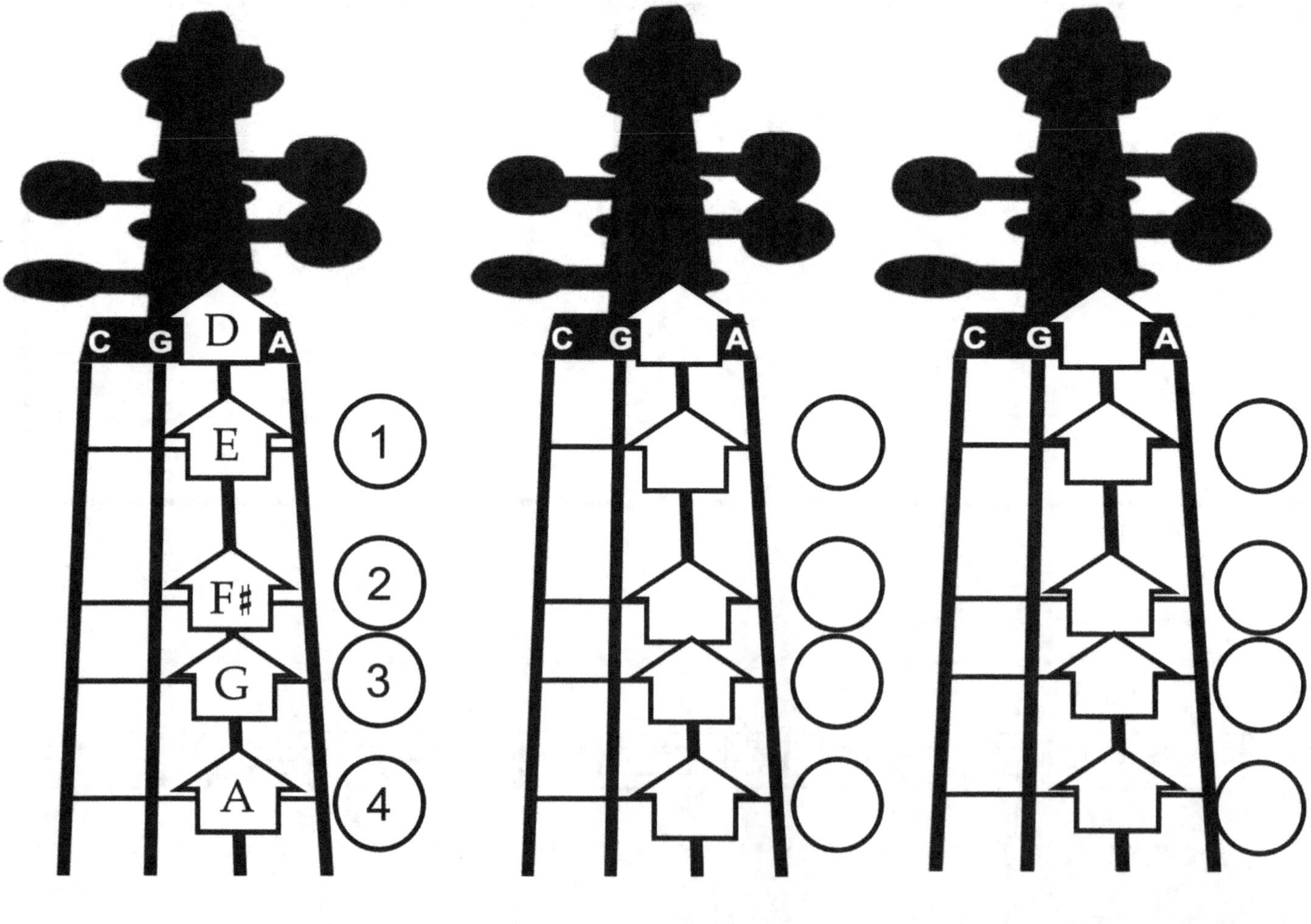

26

What do you hear? #3

You will hear 4 notes. If the 4 notes you hear are fast, circle Allegro. If the 4 notes you hear are slow, circle Adagio.

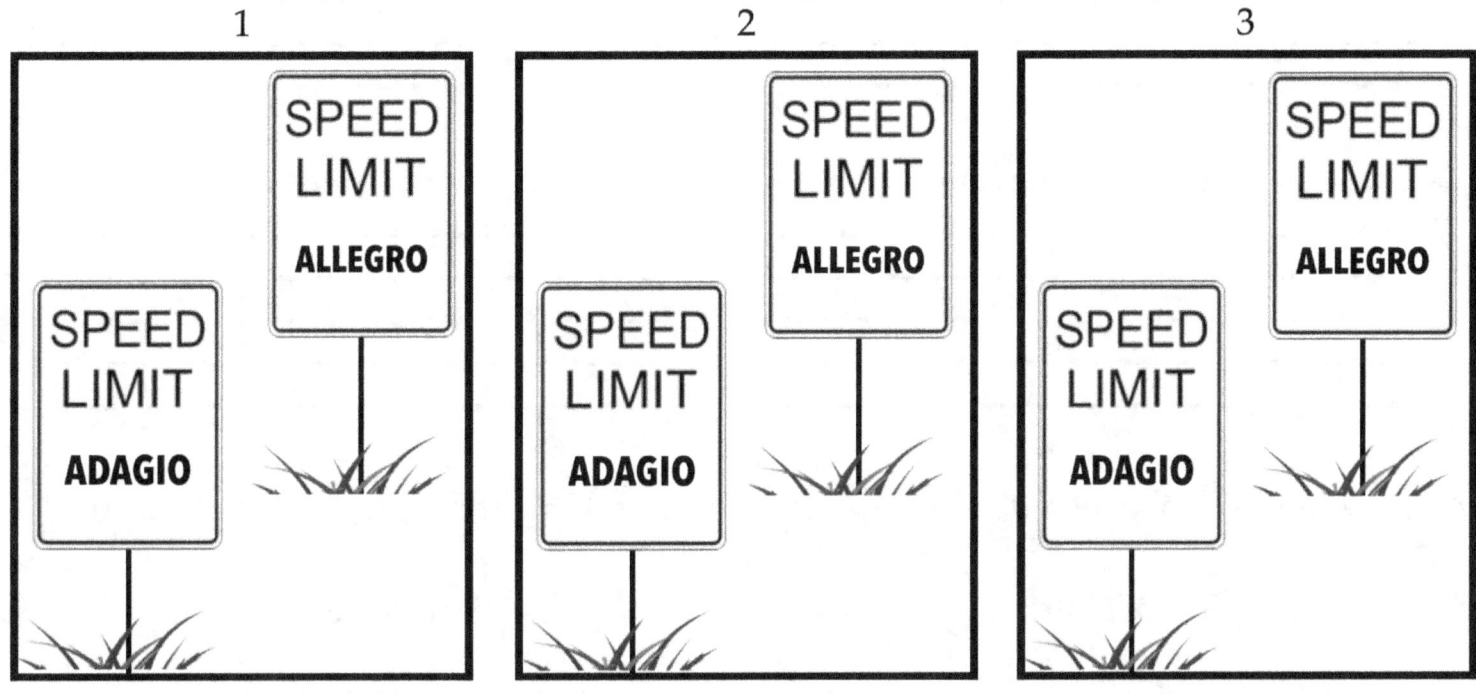

You will hear 4 notes. If the 4 notes you hear are loud, circle *f* for forte. If the 4 notes you hear are soft, circle *p* for piano.

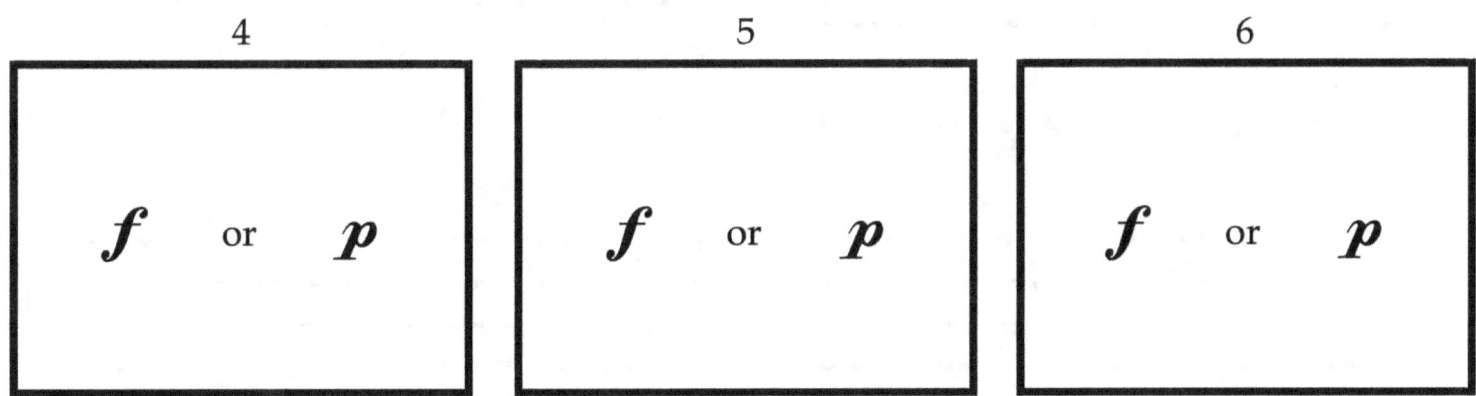

* Additional ear training exercises can be found on p. 95 & 97.

Choose from these examples for #1-3 and play it fast, or slow. For #4-6 add forte or piano to an example below.

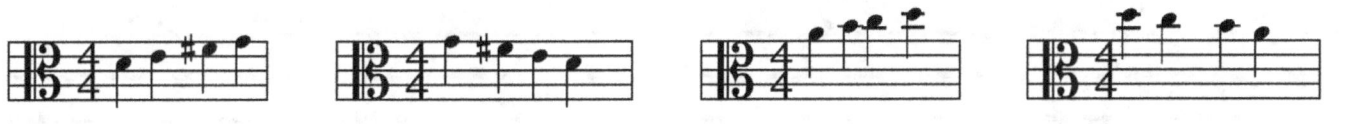

Lesson 8

This is a **staff.** The staff is made up of **5 lines and 4 spaces**. We start numbering the lines and the spaces on the lowest line or the lowest space and count up.

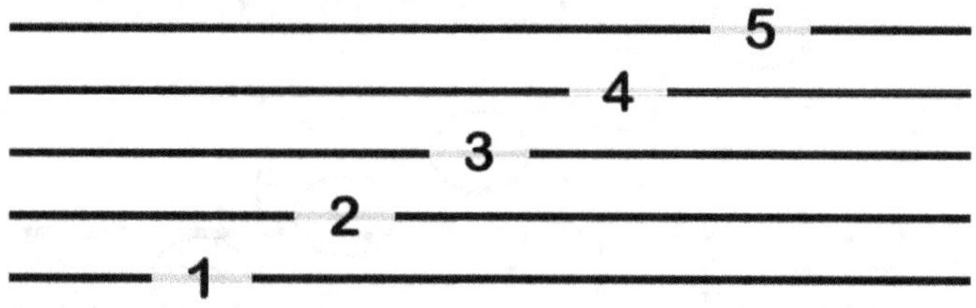

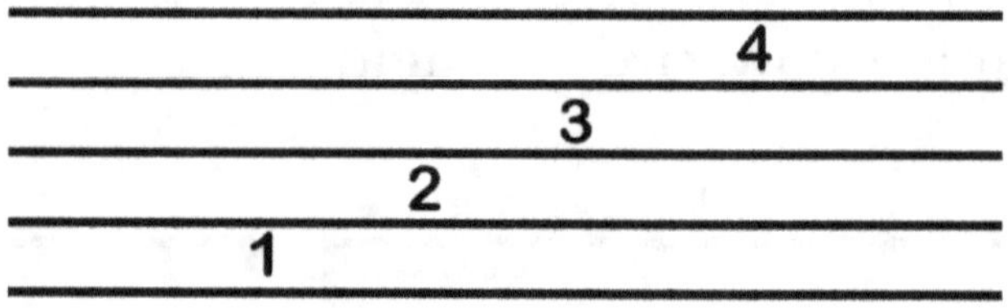

1. Write the numbers on the lines.

2. Write the numbers in the spaces.

A **space note** sits between two lines. A **line note** has a line through the middle of the note head.

Space Note

Line Note

3. Draw 3 space notes between the lines.

4. Draw 3 line notes on the line.

5. Color all the space notes green and the line notes blue.

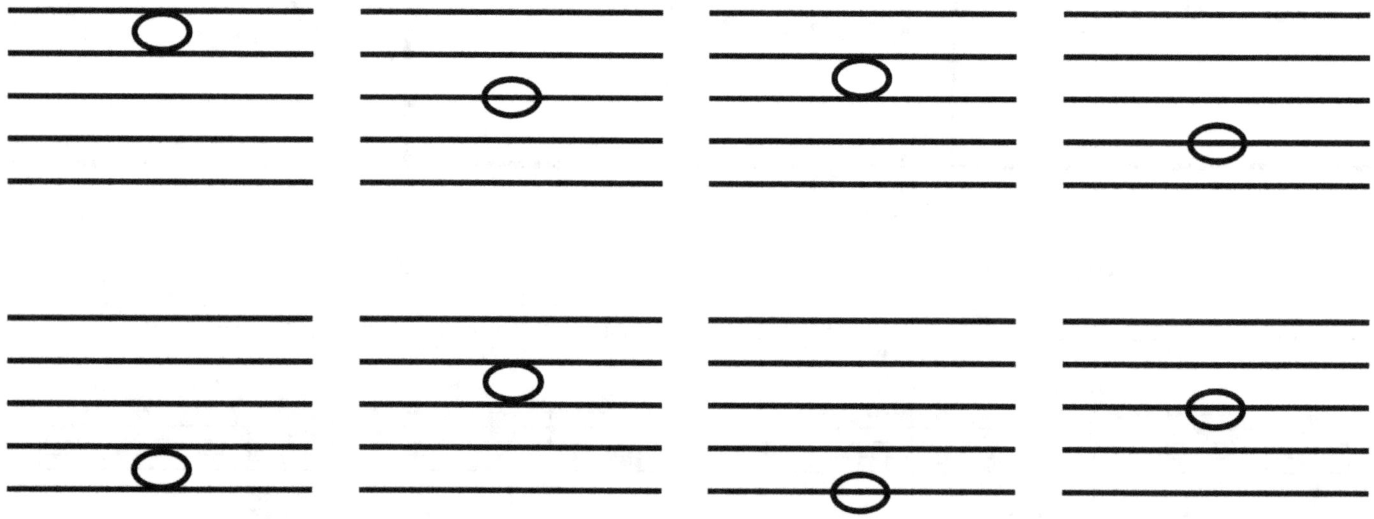

6. Write the line or space number for each note in the blank.

Line _____   Space _____   Line _____   Space _____

Line _____   Space _____   Line _____   Space _____

7. Draw the note on the correct line.

Line 3   Line 1   Line 5   Line 2

8. Draw the note in the correct space.

Space 2   Space 4   Space 3   Space 1

9. Write the total number of beats for each note in the heart.

29

Lesson 9

The violin, viola, and cello all use a different clef to read music. Violinists use the treble clef. Violists use the alto clef. Cellists and bassists use the bass clef.

Treble Clef   **Alto Clef**   **Bass Clef**

This is the **treble clef**. Treble means high. The treble clef shows the high notes on the staff. It is also called the "**G clef**" because it wraps around the "G" line on the staff. Violinists read music using the treble clef.

This is the **alto clef.** The alto clef shows the middle notes on the staff. It is also called the "**C clef**" because it points to the line on the staff where "C" lives. Violists read music using the alto clef.

This is the **bass clef.** The bass clef shows the low notes on the staff. We pronounce the name, bass like "base" in baseball, or the double bass. Sometimes it is called the "**F clef**" because it shows note "F" on the staff. Cellists and double bassists read music using this clef.

1. Color the treble clef blue, the alto clef green, and the bass clef purple.

2. Help the ranch hands round up the cows.
  • Draw a square around the quarter note cows.
  • Draw a triangle around the half note cows.
  • Draw a heart around the dotted half note cows.
  • Draw a circle around the whole note cows.

Lesson 10

How to draw an alto clef.

1. Draw each step in the empty staff.

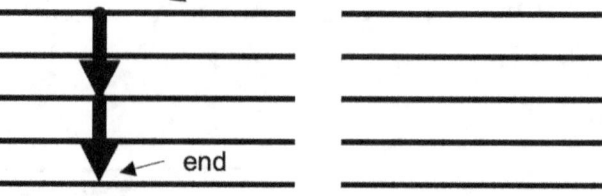

Step 1: Draw a thick line from line 5 to line 1.

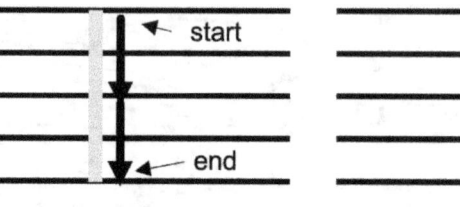

Step 2: Draw a thin line on the right side of the thick line.

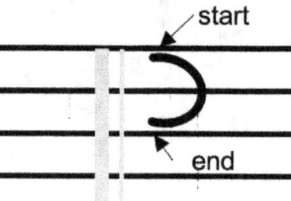

Step 3: Draw a backwards C, starting on line 5, ending in space 3. Leave a little space between the line and the C.

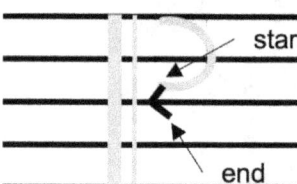

Step 4: Draw a sideways "V" with the point of the v on line 3.

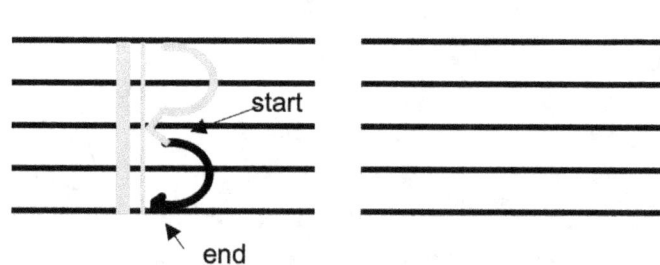

Step 5: Draw a backwards C starting at the at the end of the v in space 2.

2. Following the steps above, trace the alto clefs on each staff below.

3. Following the steps on p. 32, draw an alto clef on each staff below.

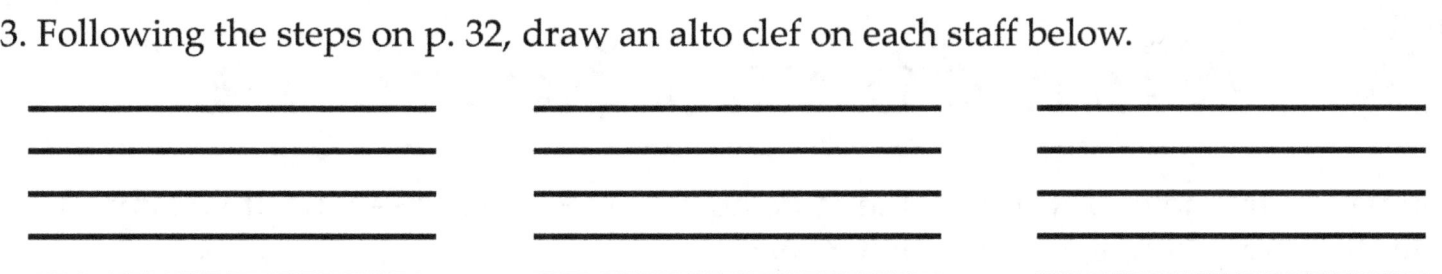

4. Draw a line matching the clef to the instrument that reads music using that clef.

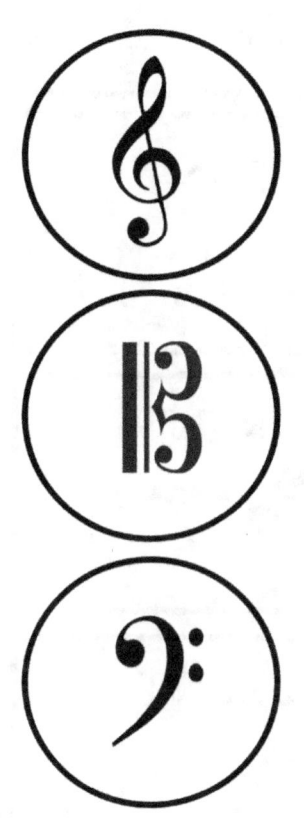

5. Circle the alto clefs that are drawn correctly. Draw an X through the alto clefs that are incorrect.

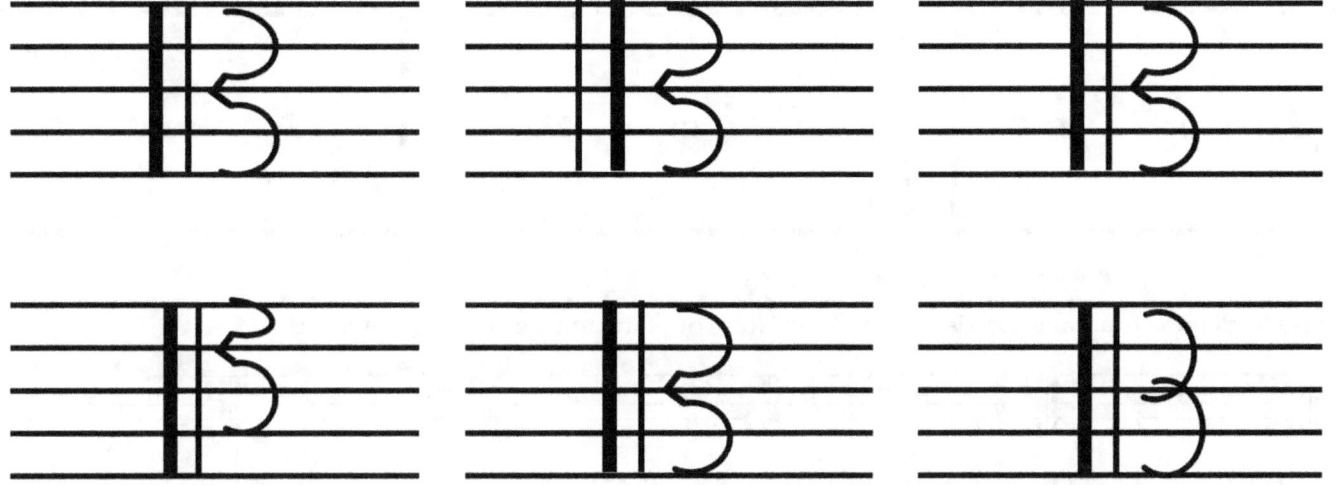

What do you hear? #4

You will hear 3 notes. If you hear the same note 3 times, circle "SAME." If you hear 3 notes that are different, circle "DIFFERENT."

1. SAME    DIFFERENT

2. SAME    DIFFERENT

3. SAME    DIFFERENT

4. SAME    DIFFERENT

Circle the dynamic you hear. If the music you hear is loud, circle *f* for forte. If the music you hear is soft, circle *p* for piano.

5	6	7
f or *p*	*f* or *p*	*f* or *p*

* Additional ear training exercises can be found on p.96 & 97.

Choose from these examples for #1-4. For #5-7 add forte or piano to an example below.

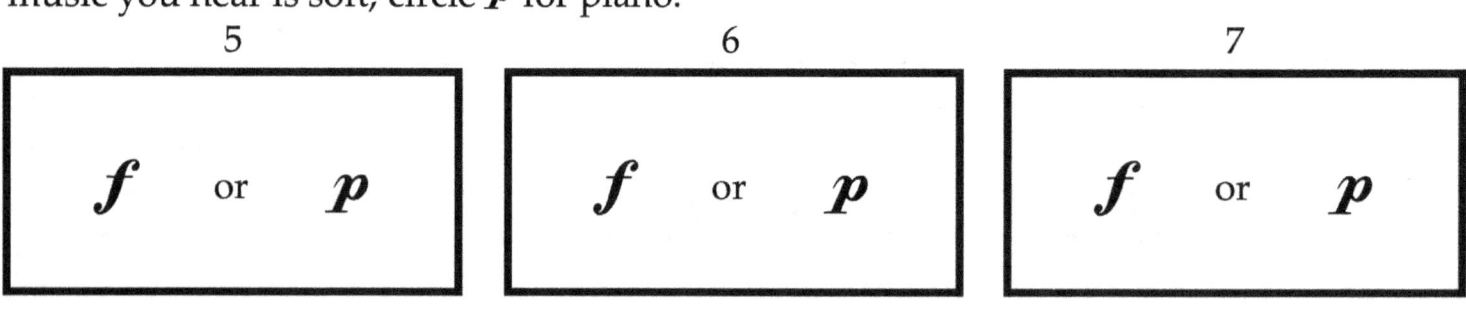

Lesson 11

1. Write one letter of the music alphabet in each leaf.

2. Draw a line from the name to the correct clef.

Alto Clef   Bass Clef   Treble Clef

3. Draw the note in the box that matches the number of beats.

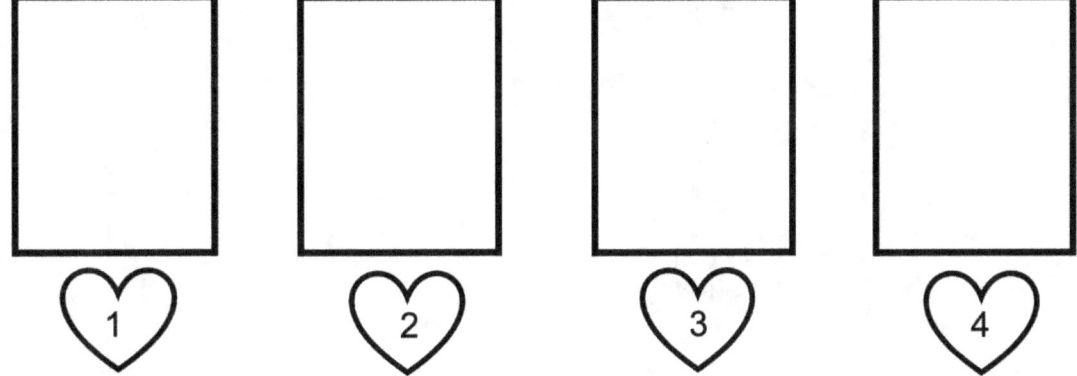

4. Write the line or space number for each note.

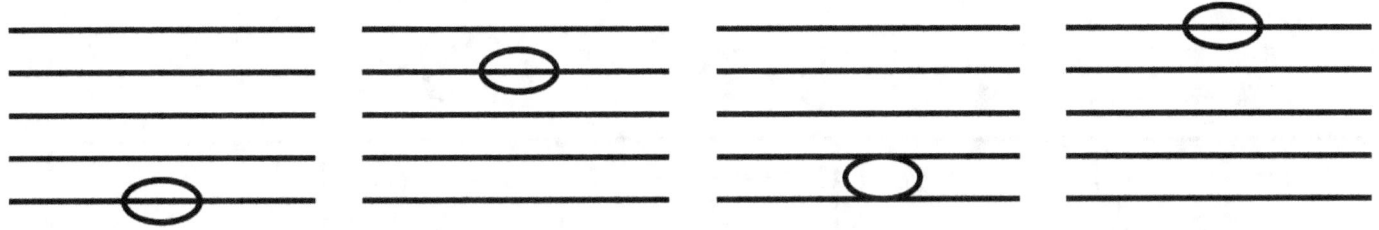

Line _____   Line _____   Space _____   Line _____

5. Forte means _____.   6. Piano means _____.

Did you know?

?? Before computers were invented, music was written by hand. Composers gave their music to a **copyist** who would neatly write out the music. The pens that were used to write music had a wide tip called a nib. These pens are sort of like calligraphy pens today. When composers drew a curved line with a wide nib, the thickness of the line would change. Composers never picked up their pen and colored the sides of the notes. It was just how the pen worked. When the typewriter and computer were invented, font designers kept the look of how copyists drew music notes and symbols with the old pens. Can you see how the thickness of the line changes with the wide nibbed pen?

thin

thick

Because your pencil has a sharp point and not a wide nib, the line for the notes you draw will not change thickness. You should not color in the sides of the notes to make them thicker. With a pencil, only draw music notes with a thin line.

1. Draw the symbol in each box with a pencil using a thin line.

Lesson 12

When we step up in the music alphabet, we move forward through the music alphabet. As we step up, the pitch moves higher. When we step down in the music alphabet, we move **backwards** through the music alphabet and the pitch goes down.

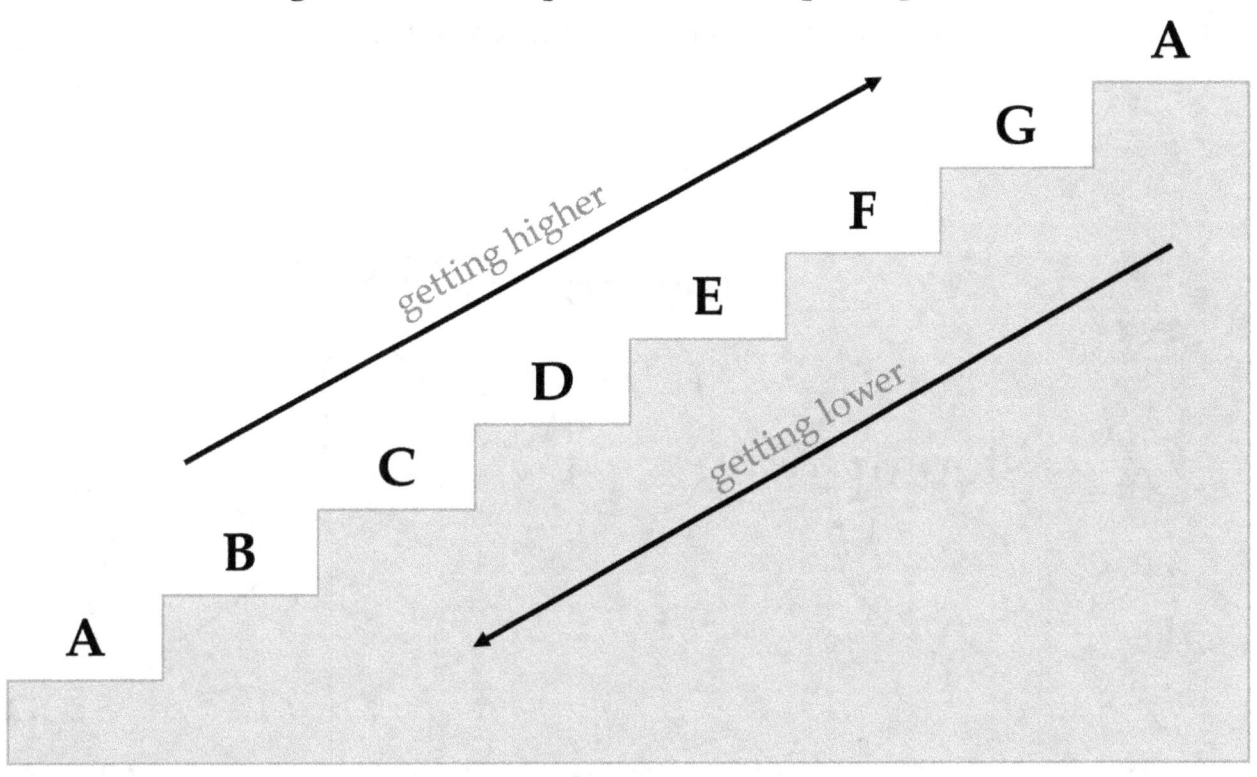

1. Fill in the blanks with the correct letter.

A – step up – land on _____   E – step down – land on _____

C – step up – land on _____   B – step down – land on _____

E – step up – land on _____   F – step down – land on _____

B – step up – land on _____   A – step down – land on _____

G – step up – land on _____   C – step down – land on _____

2. When we step up, we move _____ through the music alphabet
(forward / backward)

and the pitch goes _____. When we step down, we move _____
(up / down)   (forward / backward)

through the music alphabet and the pitch goes _____.
(up / down)

3. This little chirpy chick got lost. Can you help her find her way back to her family? Following the directions, write in the letter in each corn kernel to step up or down.

4. What letter finally got the chick home? _____

BONUS: Using your instrument, play the baby chick's path.

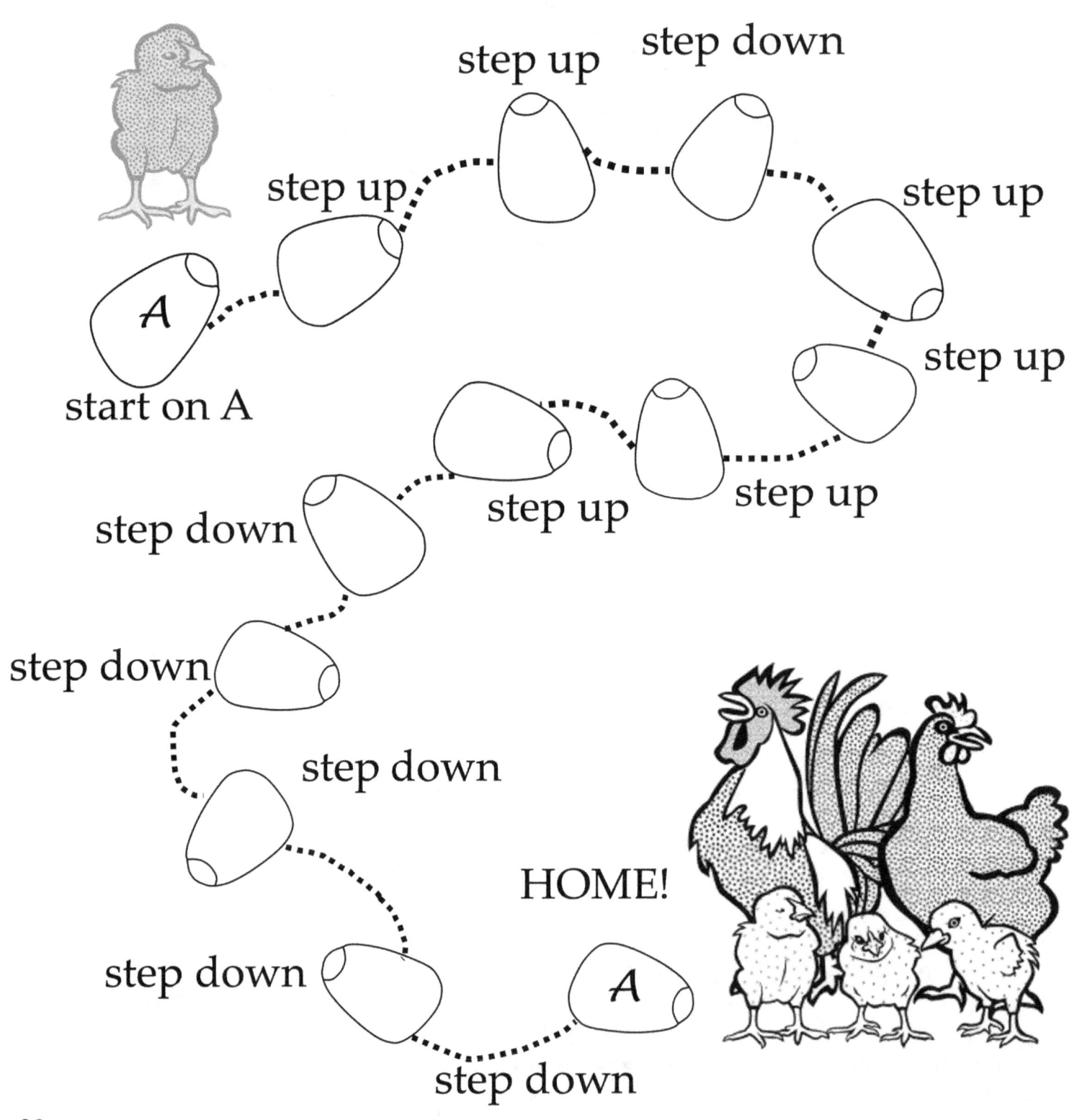

step up

step down

step up

step up

step up

step up

step up

start on A

A

step down

step up

step down

step down

step down

HOME!

step down

A

step down

Lesson 13

1. Circle if the two letters are stepping up or stepping down.

D to E = step up or step down   G to F♯ = step up or step down

B to A = step up or step down   C♯ to D = step up or step down

G to A = step up or step down   A to B = step up or step down

To step up from G we land on _____. There are two ways to play A on the viola 4th finger on the D string or with open A. **These A's are the SAME NOTE.** This is a repeated note even though they are on different places on the fingerboard! They sound the same pitch!

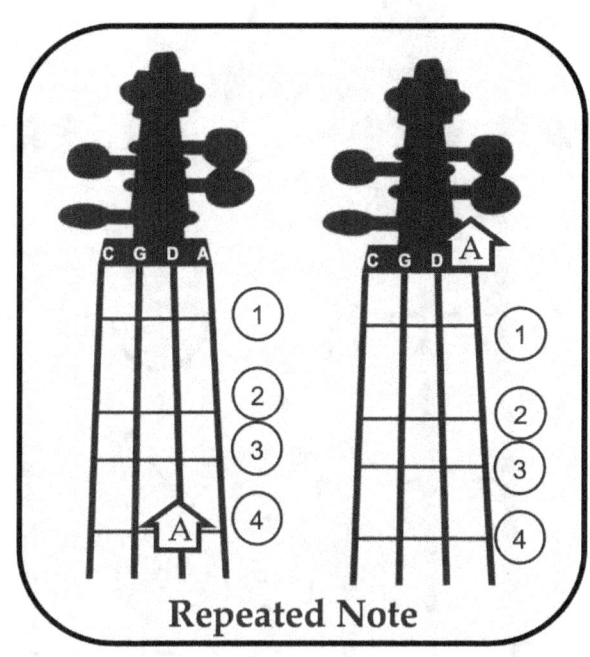

Repeated Note

2. Draw a line from the finger number on the basketball to the letter that finger plays on the D string.

Fingerboard Power! The fingers on the A string each have a letter name. As we set fingers onto the fingerboard, we go forward through the music alphabet starting on A. One letter has a sharp (♯) on the A string, C♯.

3. Write the A string letters in each house. Write the finger number in the circle.

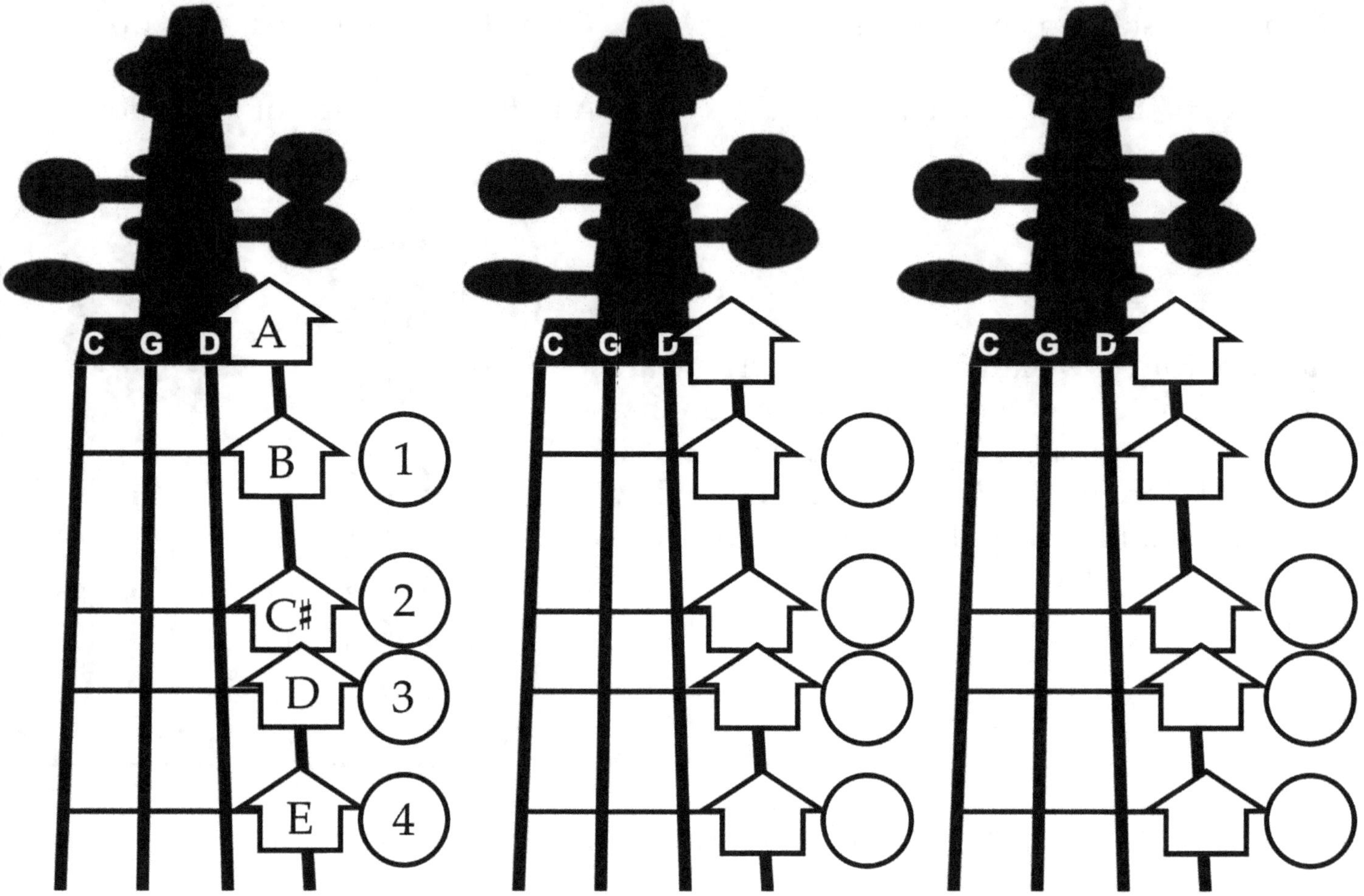

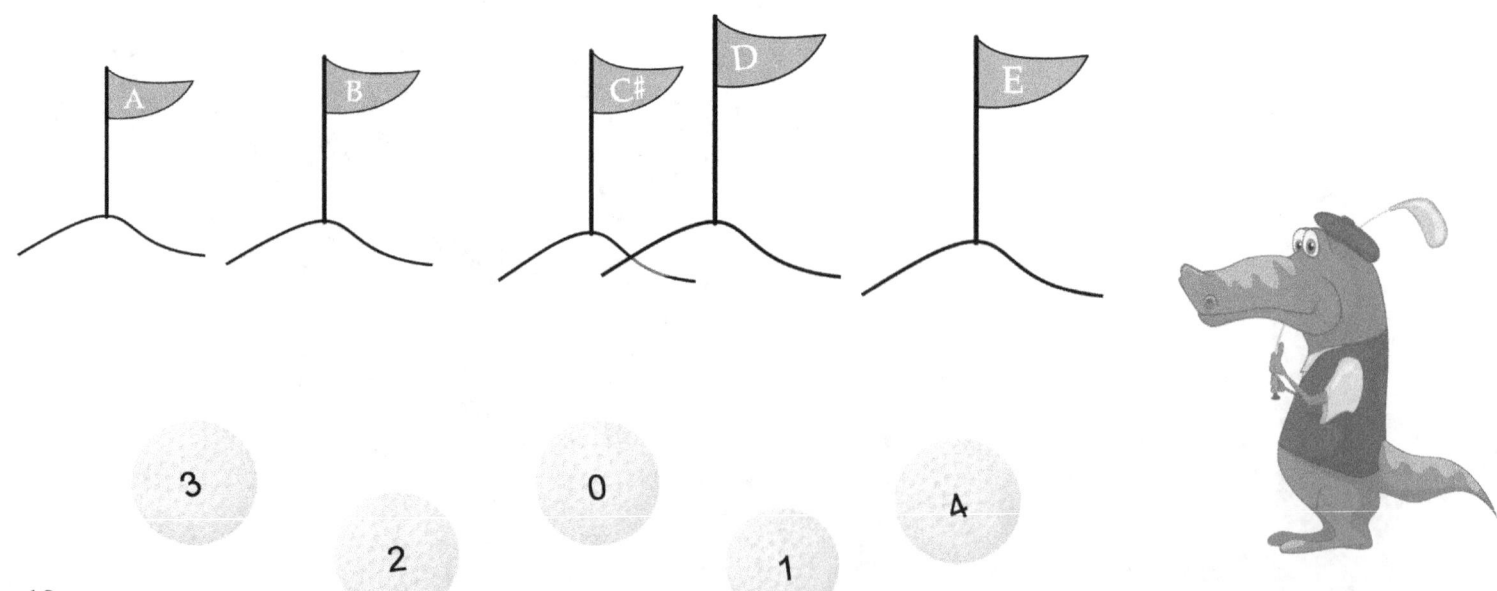

4. Help Alexander Alligator play golf. Match the golf ball with the A string finger number to the flag with the E string letter.

Lesson 14

Fingerboard Power!

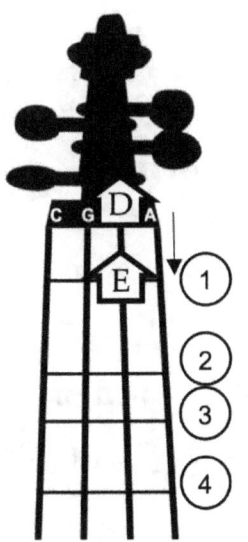

Stepping Up
To **step up** on the fingerboard, place the next finger onto the fingerboard.

Stepping Down
To **step down** on the fingerboard, lift a finger off the fingerboard.

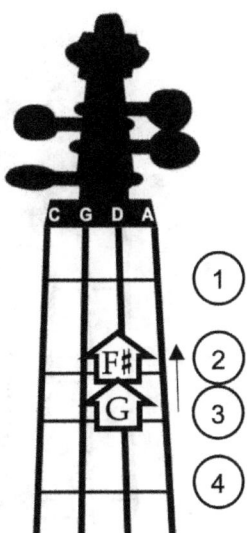

1. On the fingerboard, draw a circle that is a *step up* from the letter in the house. Then, write the letter name in the circle. Finally, fill in the blanks in the gray box.

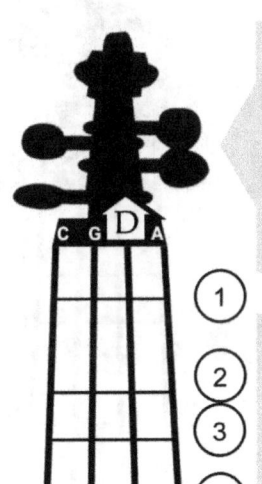

Letter: D – step up – land on _____

Finger: ___0___ – step up – play finger _____.

Letter: E – step up – land on _____

Finger: _____ – step up – play finger _____.

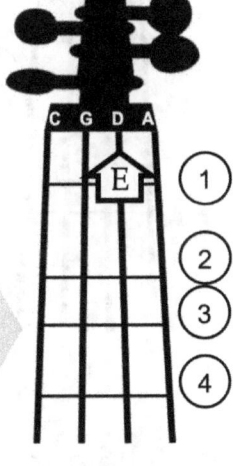

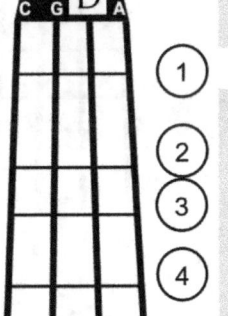

Letter: F♯ – step up – land on _____

Finger: _____ – step up – play finger _____.

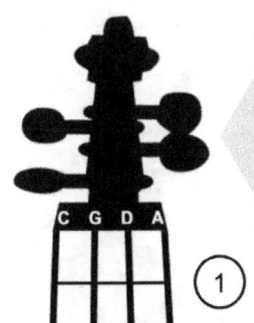

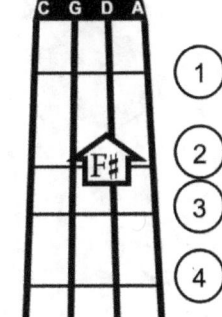

Letter: G – step up – land on _____

Finger: _____ – step up – play finger _____.

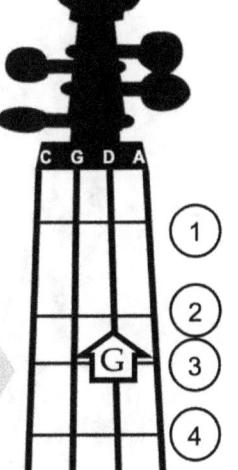

2. On the fingerboard, draw a circle that is a *step down* from the letter in the house. Then, write the letter name in the circle. Finally, fill in the blanks in the gray box.

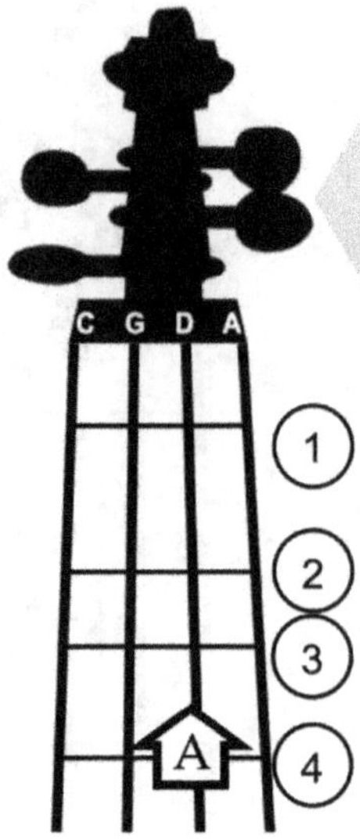

Letter: A – step down – land on _____

Finger: __4__ – step down – play finger ____.

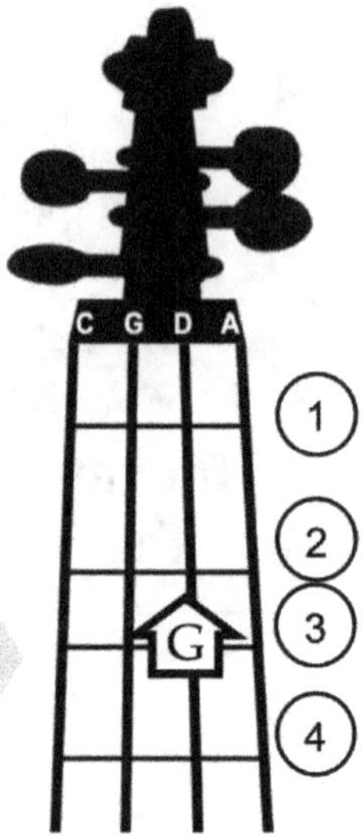

Letter: G – step down – land on _____

Finger: ____ – step down – play finger ____.

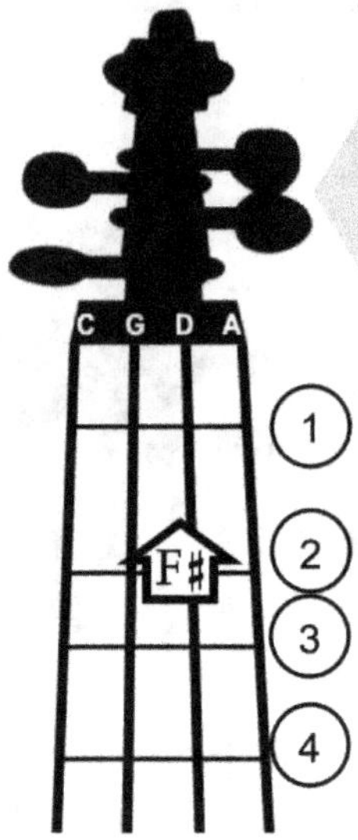

Letter: F♯ – step down – land on _____

Finger: ____ – step down – play finger ____.

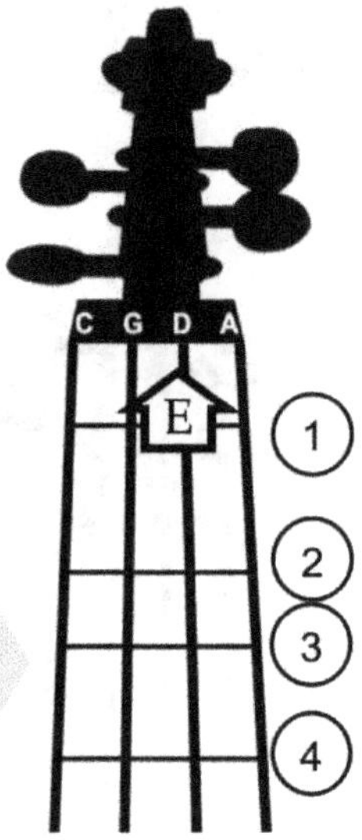

Letter: B – step down – land on _____

Finger: ____ – step down – play finger ____.

3. Watch your step! Fill in the missing letters.

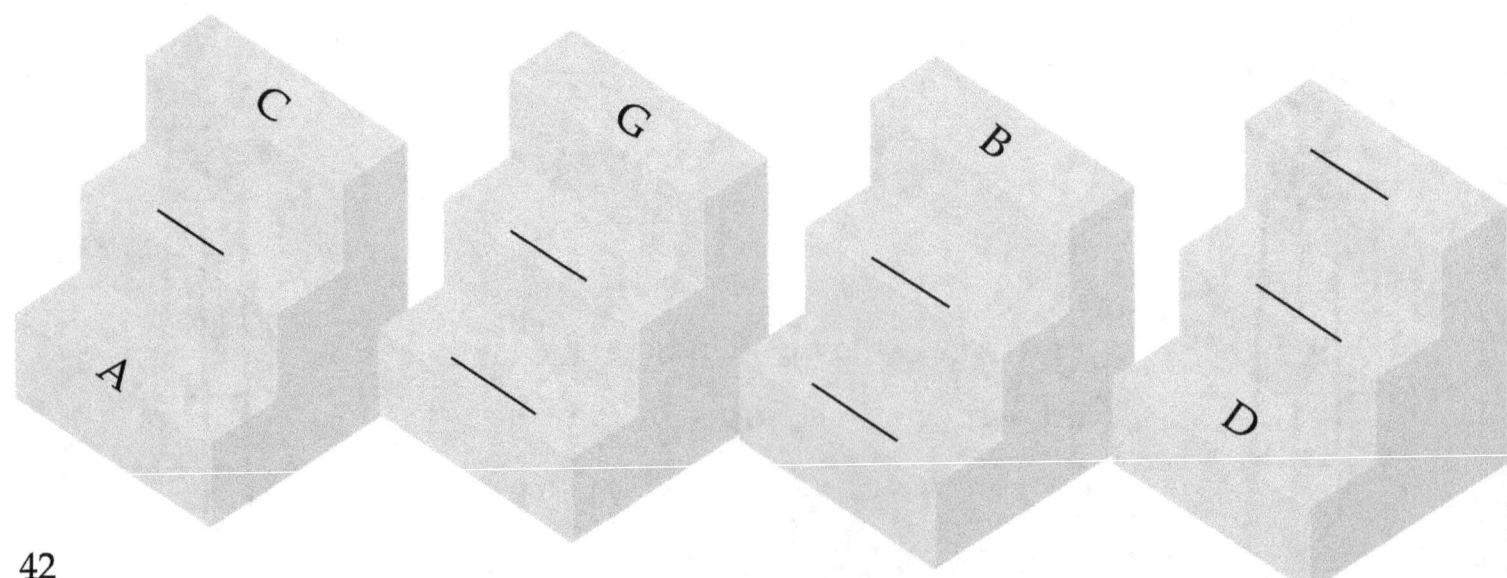

Lesson 15

1. Fill in the gray box. Then, on the fingerboard draw a circle that is a *step up* or a *step down* from the letter in the house. Finally, write the letter name in the circle.

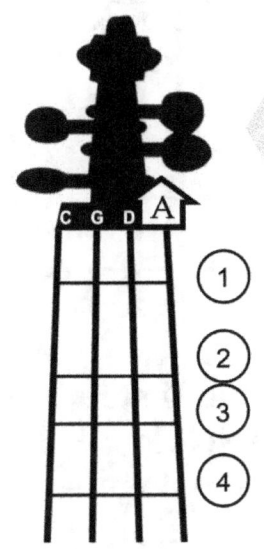

Letter: A – **step up** – land on _____

Finger: __0__ – **step up** – play finger ____.

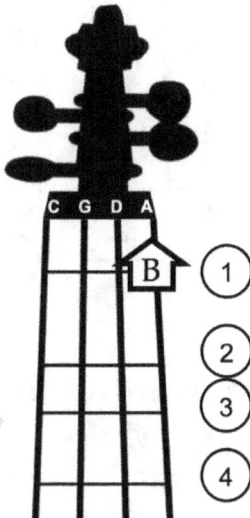

Letter: B – **step up** – land on _____

Finger: ____ – **step up** – play finger ____.

Letter: C♯ – **step up** – land on _____

Finger: ____ – **step up** – play finger ____.

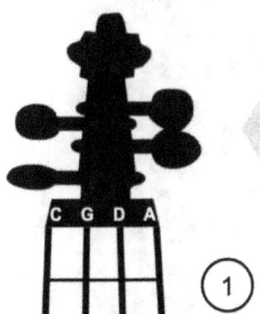

Letter: D – **step up** – land on _____

Finger: ____ – **step up** – play finger ____.

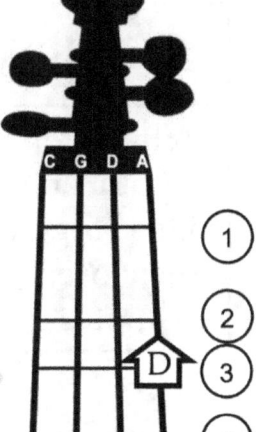

Letter: E – **step down** – land on _____

Finger: __4__ – **step down** – play finger ____.

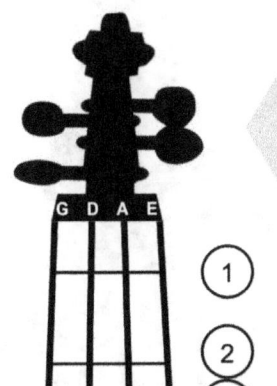

Letter: D – **step down** – land on _____

Finger: ____ – **step down** – play finger ____.

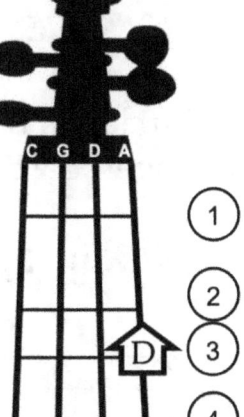

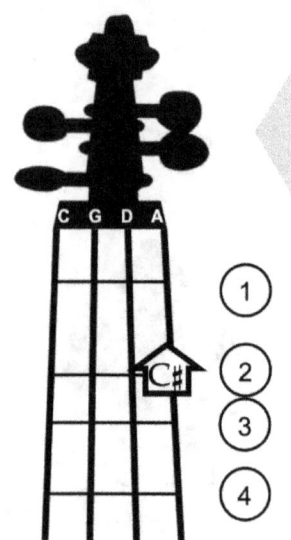

Letter: C# – **step down** – land on _____

Finger: _____ – **step down** – play finger _____.

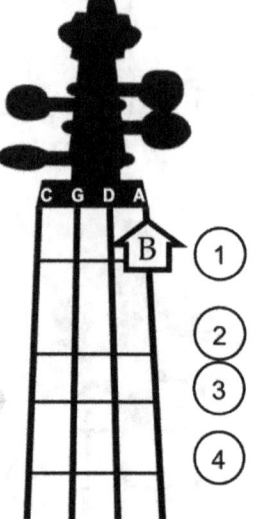

Letter: B – **step down** – land on _____

Finger: _____ – **step down** – play finger _____.

Steps are always one finger to the next finger. There are 2 kinds of steps, a **half step** and a **whole step.** A half step is the smallest step. It is when the fingers are close together. A whole step is 2 half steps together and there is space between the fingers.

Half Step
A half step is when your fingers are close together. It is the closest that two notes can be.

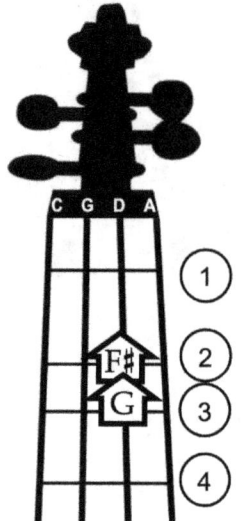

Whole Step
A whole step is 2 half steps together. There is a space between your fingers.

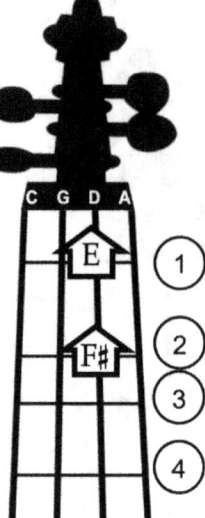

2. Circle the finger numbers that are a half step on the fingerboard picture.

     1 & 2   **2 & 3**   **3 & 4**

3. Circle the finger numbers that are a whole step on the fingerboard picture.

     1 & 2   **2 & 3**   **3 & 4**

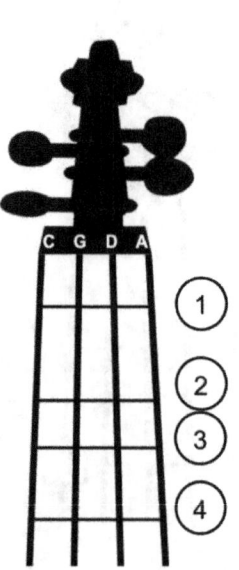

 **?? Did you know?**
An open string up to the 1st finger tape is also a whole step, even though it only uses 1 finger!

Lesson 16

Stepping on the staff

Notes can step up and down on the staff. When a note steps up on the staff, it moves from a space to the next line, or from a line to the next space.

step up
space note to line note

step up
line note to space note

(space 3, step up, line 4)   (line 3, step up, space 3)

When a note steps down on the staff, it moves from a space to the next line, or a line to the next space.

step down
space note to line note

step down
line note to space note

(space 2, step down, line 2)   (line 2, step down, space 1)

1. Draw a note below that steps UP from the given note.

2. Draw a note below that steps DOWN from the given note.

A **repeated note** stays on the same line or space.

same space   **same line**

3. Following the directions at the top of each box, draw a circle on the fingerboard that steps up or steps down from the house. Then write the letter for the printed house in the first blank. Write the letter for the circle in the second blank.

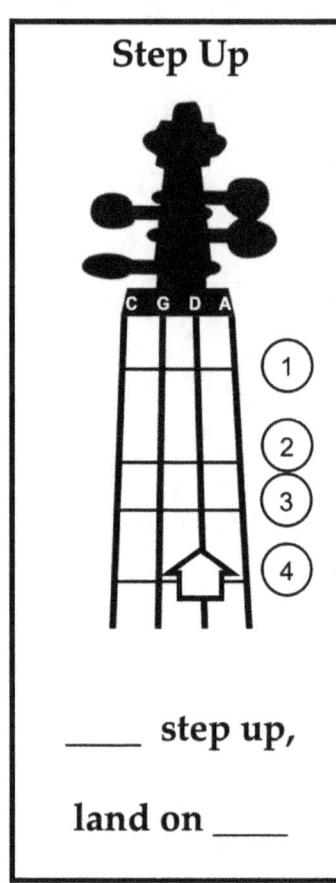

_____ step up,

land on _____

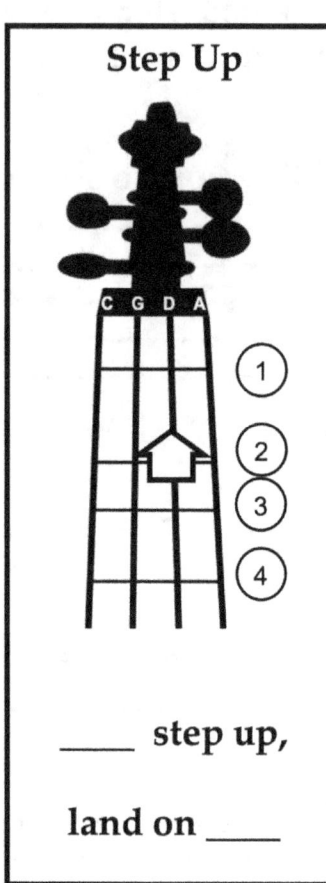

_____ step up,

land on _____

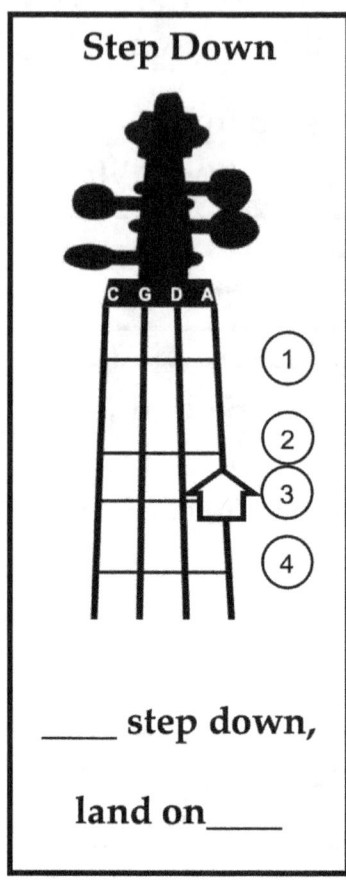

_____ step down,

land on_____

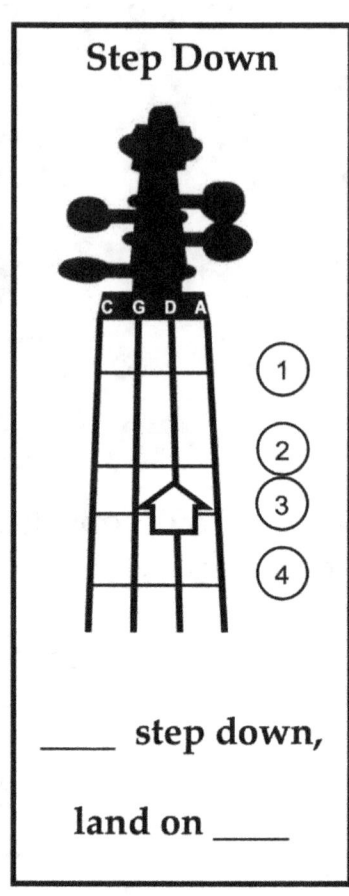

_____ step down,

land on _____

4. Draw a whole note on the line or space listed under each staff. Then, draw another whole note that steps up, steps down, or repeats.

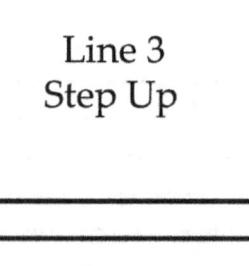

Line 3
Step Up

Space 1
Step Down

Space 3
Step Up

Line 1
Repeating

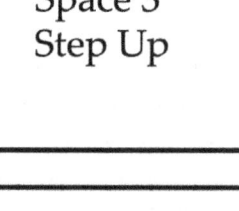

Line 4
Step Up

Line 2
Step Down

Space 4
Step Up

Space 3
Repeating

What do you hear? #5

Place a coin in each circle. You will hear 4 notes for each question. If the notes you hear step up, push the coin up to the sky. If the notes you hear step down, push the coin down to the ground.

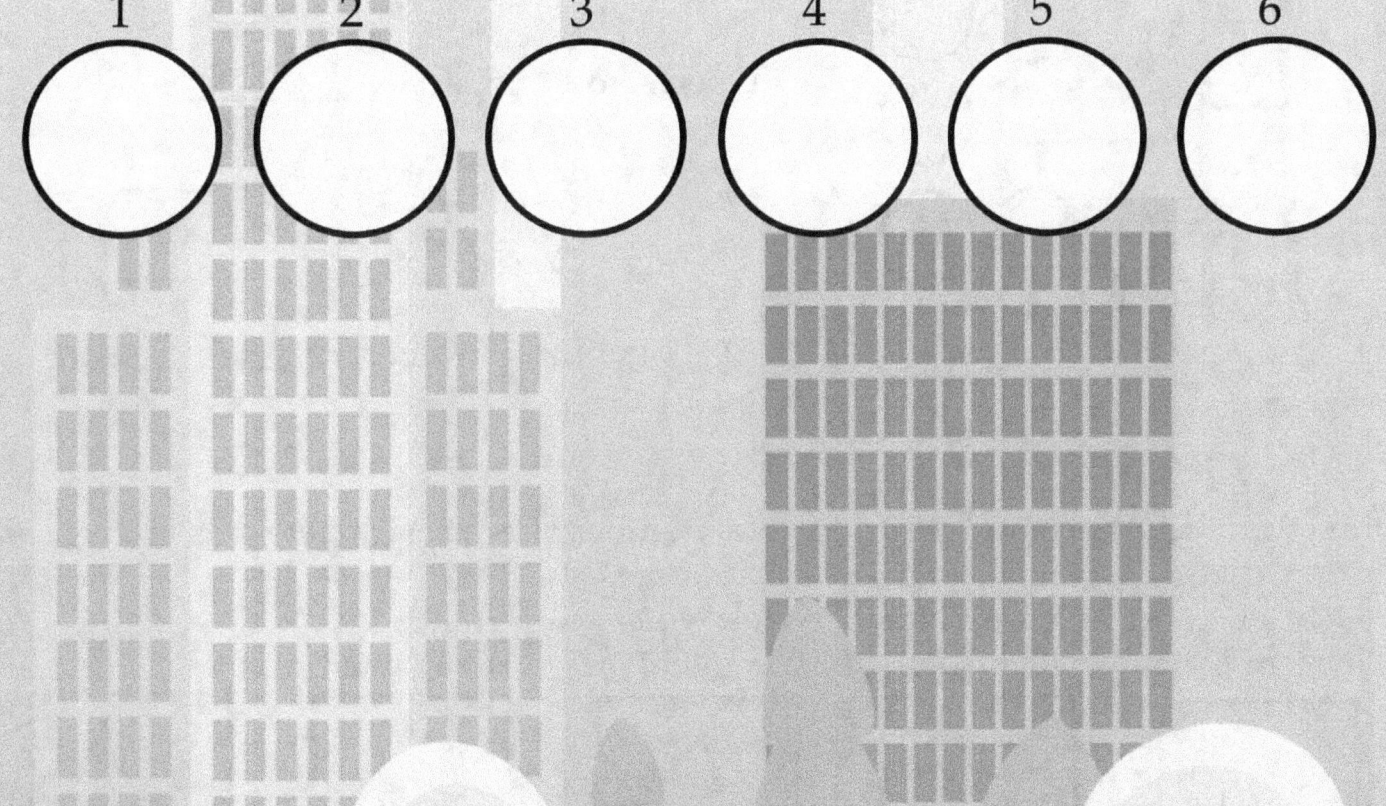

1 2 3 4 5 6

Choose from these examples:

Lesson 17

1. Write the letter for each house on the D string and A string. Then, write the finger number in the circle.

Half Step	**Whole Step**
Fingers are close together.	Space between fingers.

2. Write W if distance between the notes is a whole step. Write H if the distance between the notes is a half step.

Open D to 1st finger E = _____

1st finger E to 2nd finger F♯ = _____

2nd finger F♯ to 3rd finger G = _____

3rd finger G to 4th finger A = _____

Open A to 1st finger B = _____

1st finger B to 2nd finger C♯ = _____

2nd finger C♯ to 3rd finger D = _____

3rd finger D to 4th finger E = _____

3. Draw the note in each box. Write the total number of beats each note gets in the heart.

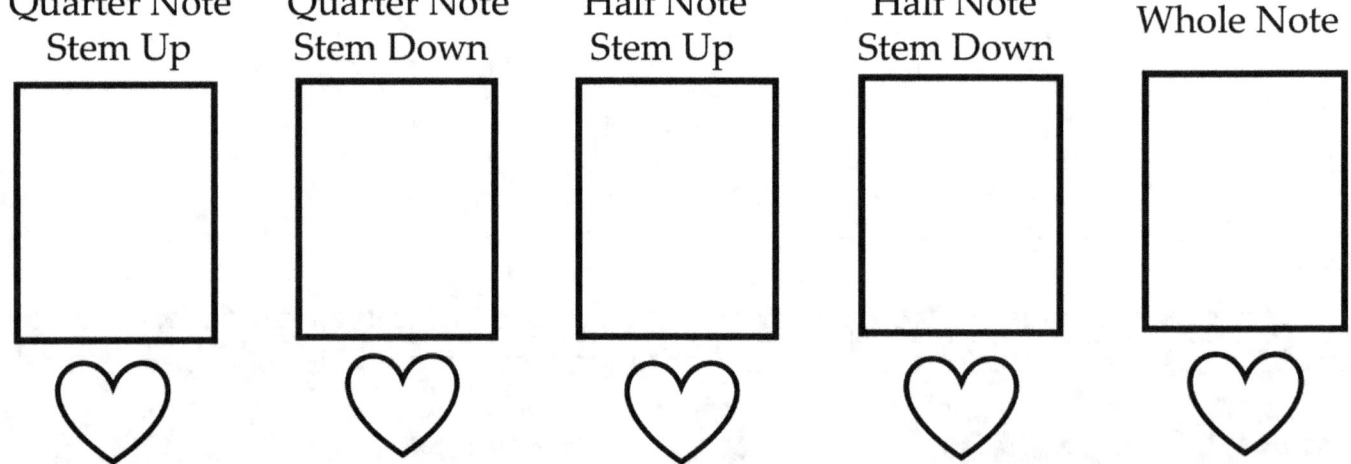

Quarter Note Stem Up Quarter Note Stem Down Half Note Stem Up Half Note Stem Down Whole Note

4. If the houses on the fingerboard are a half step, write "H" in the blank. If the houses are a whole step write, "W" in the blank.

C G D A
1
2
3
4

_____ _____ _____ _____

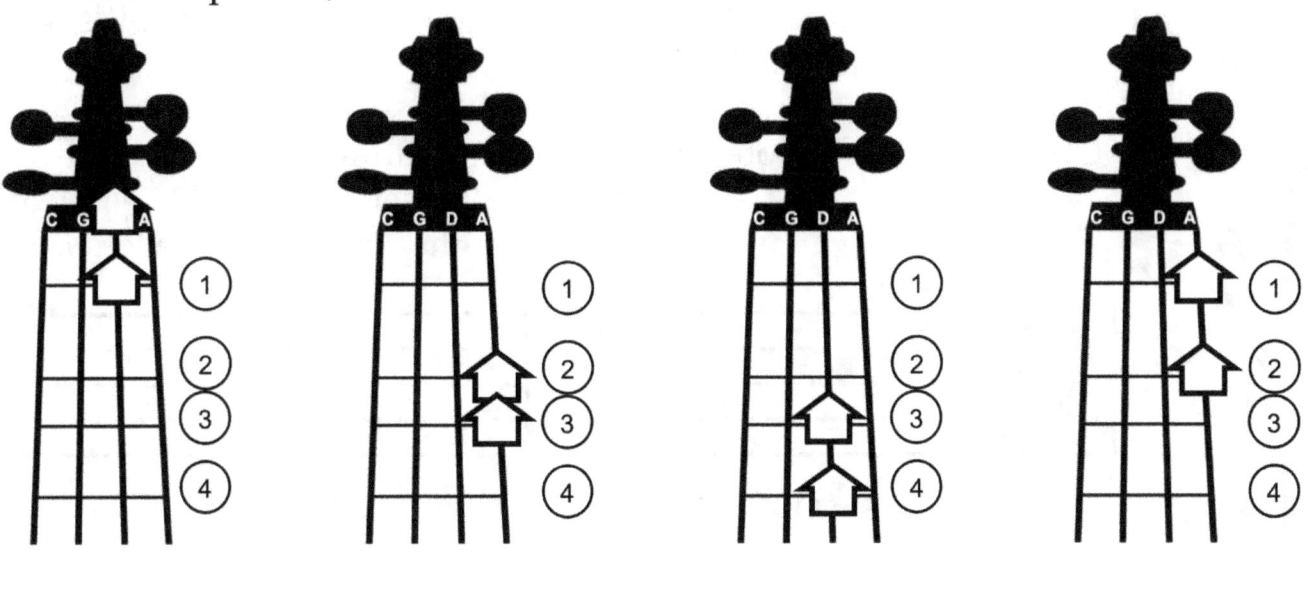

5. Circle the hidden music notes and clefs in the picture.

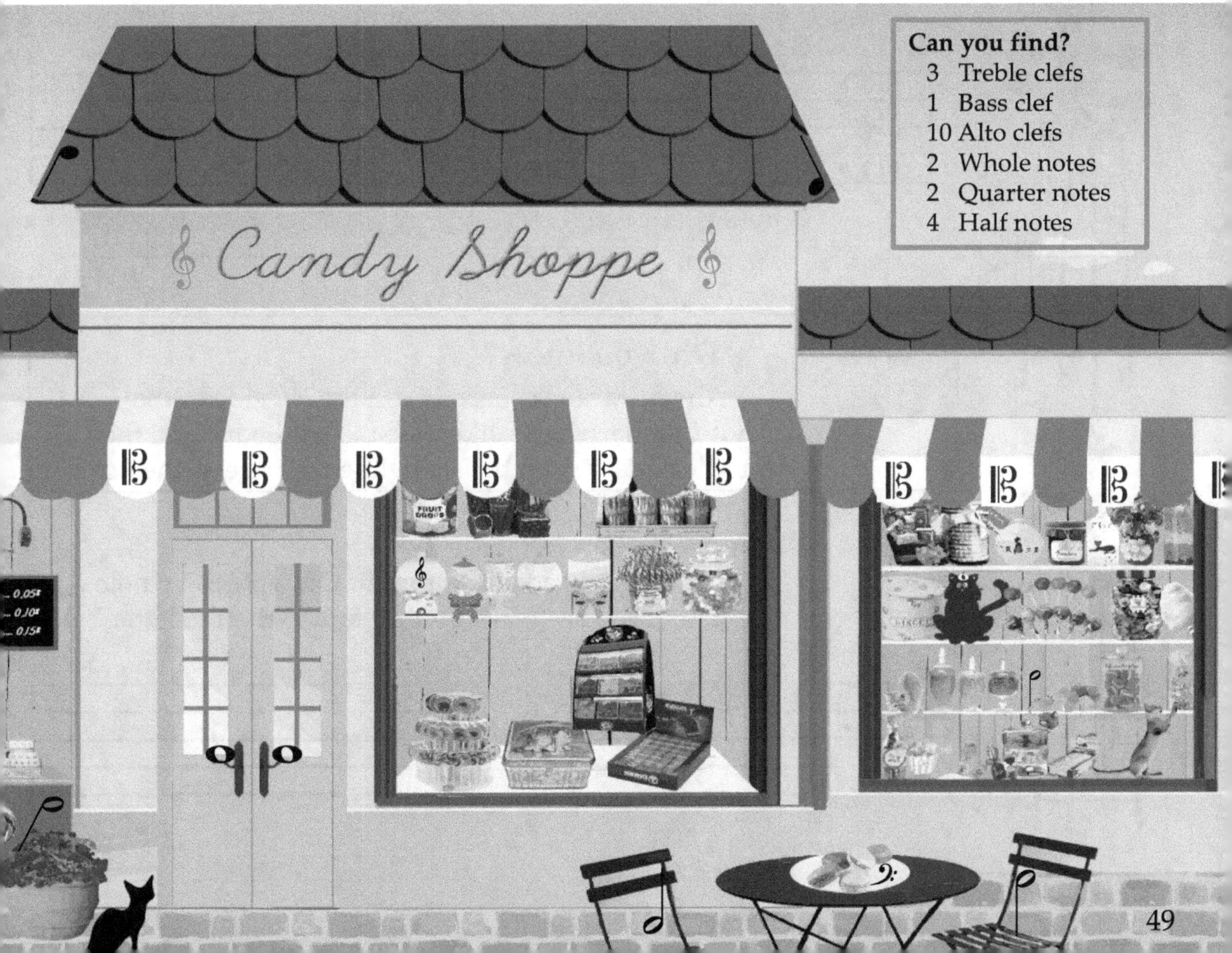

Can you find?
3 Treble clefs
1 Bass clef
10 Alto clefs
2 Whole notes
2 Quarter notes
4 Half notes
Candy Shoppe

Lesson 18

Each pitch has a house on the fingerboard and a matching house on the staff. We use notes to show the staff house of each pitch.

Open D is a space note and lives on the staff in space 3.

1. Trace the alto clef. Draw 3 "D" whole notes on the staff. Write the letter below.

Space 3 = Open D

____ ____ ____

D (space 3) – step up – land on E (line 4).

2. Trace the alto clef. Draw 3 "E" whole notes on the staff. Write the letter below.

Line 4 = E

____ ____ ____

Did you know?

?? Always draw a sharp (♯) on the *left* side of the note. A sharp looks like a tic-tac-toe board and the middle square is on the same line or space as the note.

E (line 4) – step up – land on F♯ (space 4).

3. Trace the alto clef. Draw 3 "F♯" whole notes on the staff. Write the letter below.

Space 4 = F♯

____ ____ ____

F# (space 4) – step up – land on **G** (line 5).

4. Trace the alto clef. Draw 3 "G" whole notes on the staff. Write the letter below.

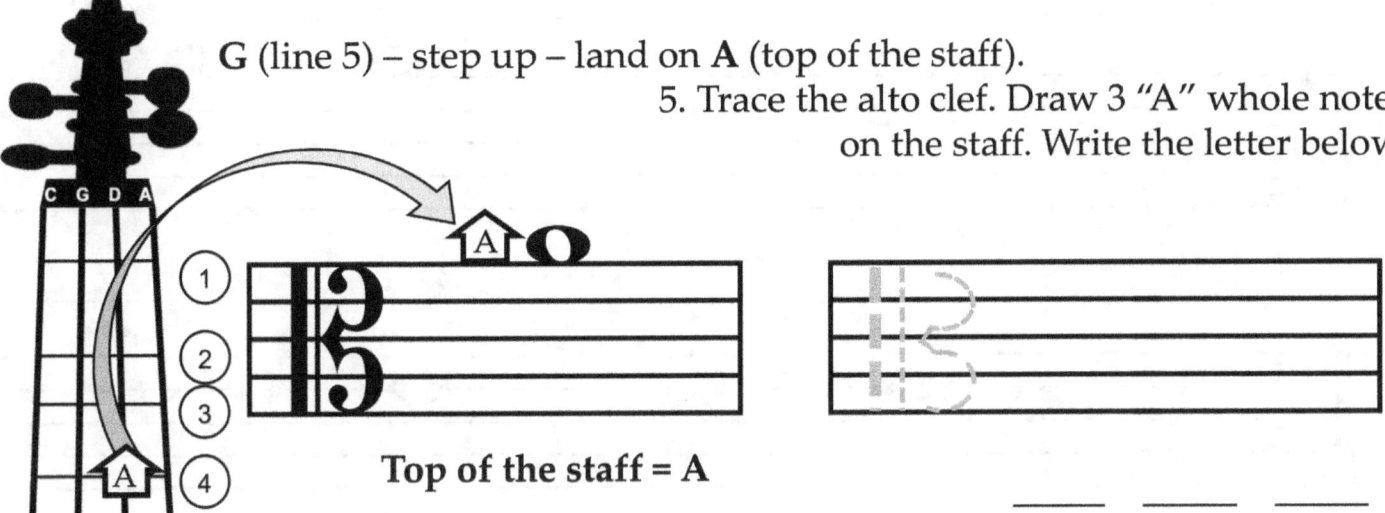

Line 5 = G

___ ___ ___

G (line 5) – step up – land on **A** (top of the staff).

5. Trace the alto clef. Draw 3 "A" whole notes on the staff. Write the letter below.

Top of the staff = A

___ ___ ___

6. Trace the alto clef. Draw the 5 D string notes on the staff. Write the finger number on the line under each note.

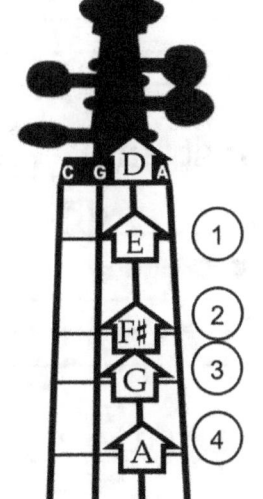

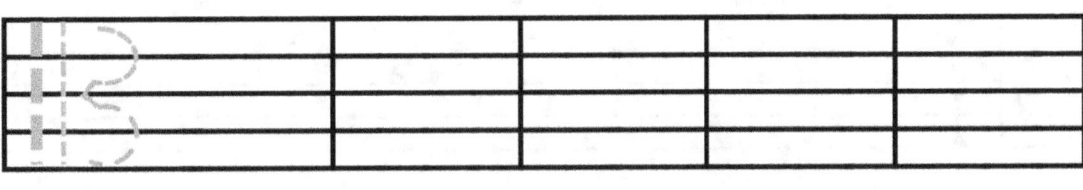

Letter Name: D   E   F#   G   A

Finger Number: ____   ____   ____   ____   ____

Discover the Composers

7. Fill in the letter of each note to learn about the life of a great composer.
   ***Hint: if there is no sharp by the note, write the letter alone.

Joh____nn S____b____stian B____ch was ____ ____r____at

compos____r. He b____ ____ ____n writin____ music wh____n

h____ was 18 y____ ____rs ol____. B____ch h____ ____

20 chil____r____n. B____ c____us____ th____y ____ll

l____ ____ne____ to pl____y ____ music____l instrum____nt,

the B____ chs h____ ____ a ____ ____mily orch____str____!

8. Name a piece you have played by this composer:_____

52

9. Follow the color code and color Patricia Panda while you listen to Johann Sebastian Bach's Sonata No. 3 in G minor for Viola da Gamba and Harpsichord I. Vivace, BWV 1029.

Color Code:
   D = Pink
   E = Gray
   F♯ = Brown
   G = Black

Lesson 19

1. Write in the letters for each D string house.

2. Write the finger in each circle.

3. Fill in the blanks under each note.

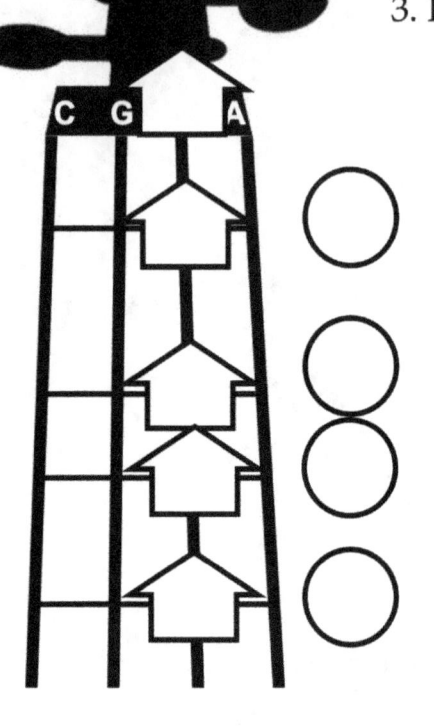

Space Number _____

Letter _____

Finger Number _____

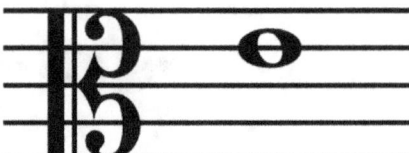

Line Number _____

Letter _____

Finger Number _____

Space Number _____

Letter _____

Finger Number _____

Line Number _____

Letter _____

Finger Number _____

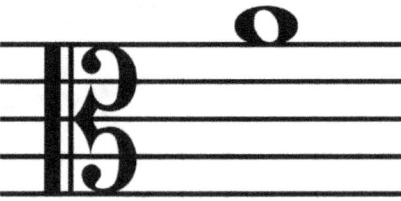

Space Number _____

Letter _____

Finger Number _____

True   or   False   4. A half step is when your fingers are far apart.

True   or   False   5. A whole step is when your fingers are far apart.

True   or   False   6. On the D string - G up to A is a whole step.

True   or   False   7. On the D string - E up to F♯ is a whole step.

True   or   False   8. On the D string – F♯ up to G is a whole step.

9. Draw an alto clef on each blank staff.

10. Write the number of beats in each heart.

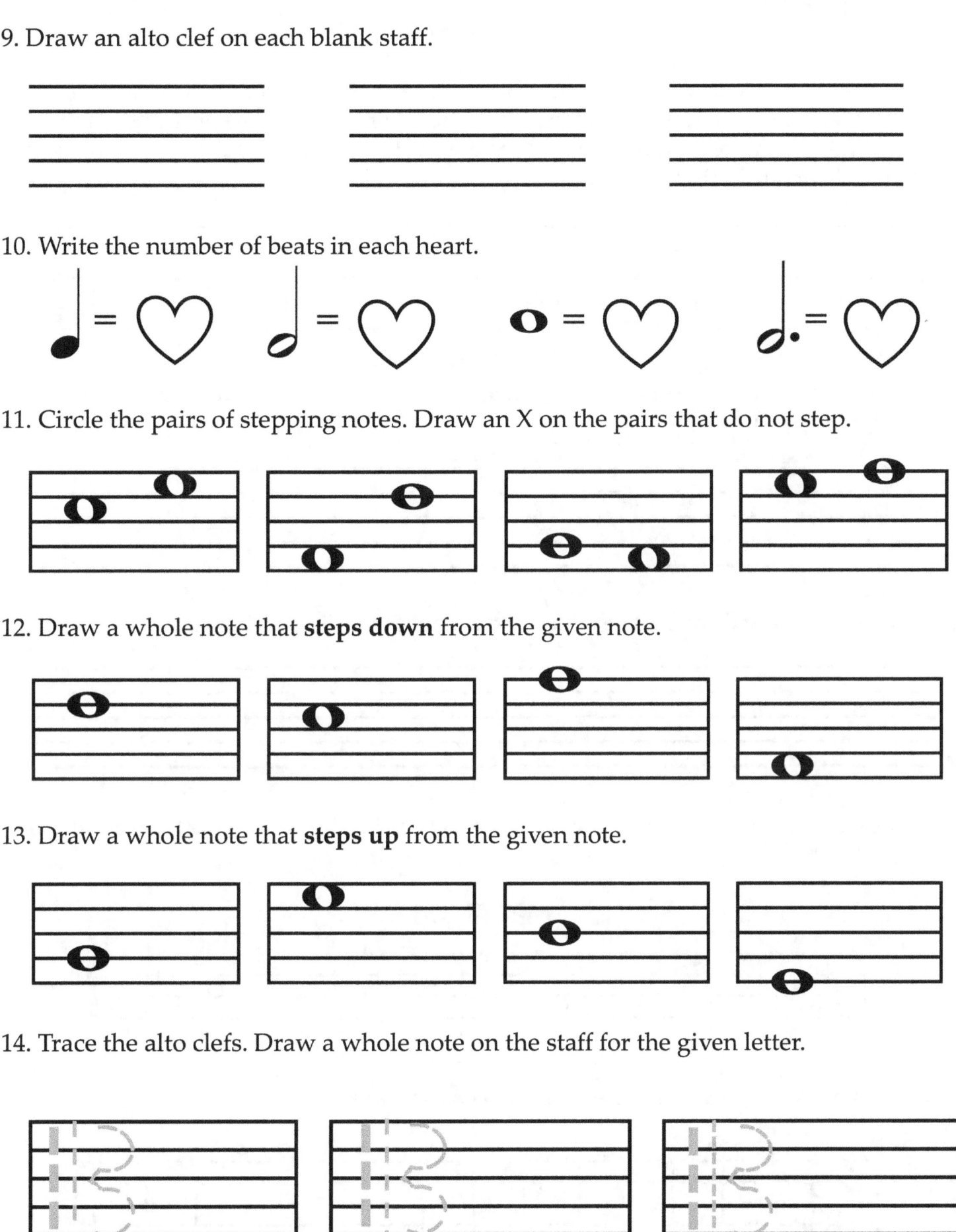

11. Circle the pairs of stepping notes. Draw an X on the pairs that do not step.

12. Draw a whole note that **steps down** from the given note.

13. Draw a whole note that **steps up** from the given note.

14. Trace the alto clefs. Draw a whole note on the staff for the given letter.

D   F♯   A

Lesson 20

The staff lines are divided by **bar lines.** The space between the bar lines is called a **measure.** Bar lines start at line 5 and end at line 1. There is a bar line at the beginning of each staff. At the end of a piece, you will see a **double bar line.** A **double bar line** is a thin line followed by a thick line.

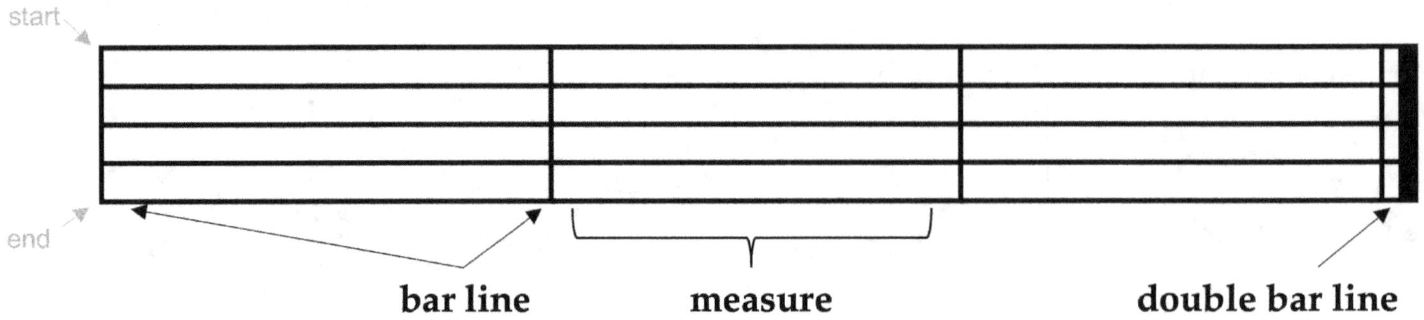

start

end

bar line   **measure**   **double bar line**

1. Trace the dots to draw bar lines and create measures.

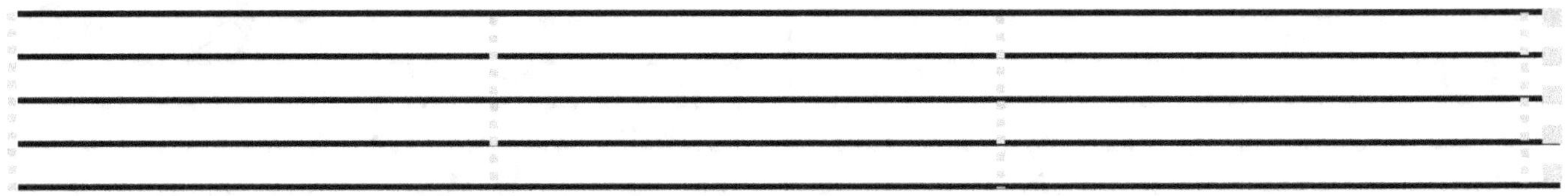

2. On the staff below draw in 3 bar lines and a double bar line at the end.

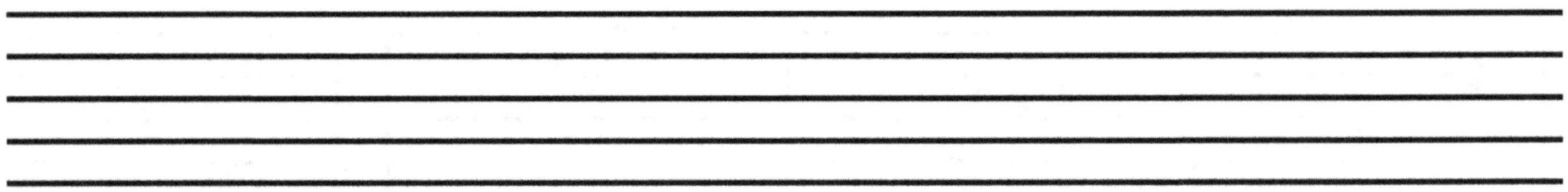

3. On the staff below, draw an arrow pointing to each bar line. Draw a box around the double bar line.

4. On the staff below, draw a circle around each measure.

5. How many measures did you circle? _____

6. Draw a circle on the fingerboard that matches the note on the staff.

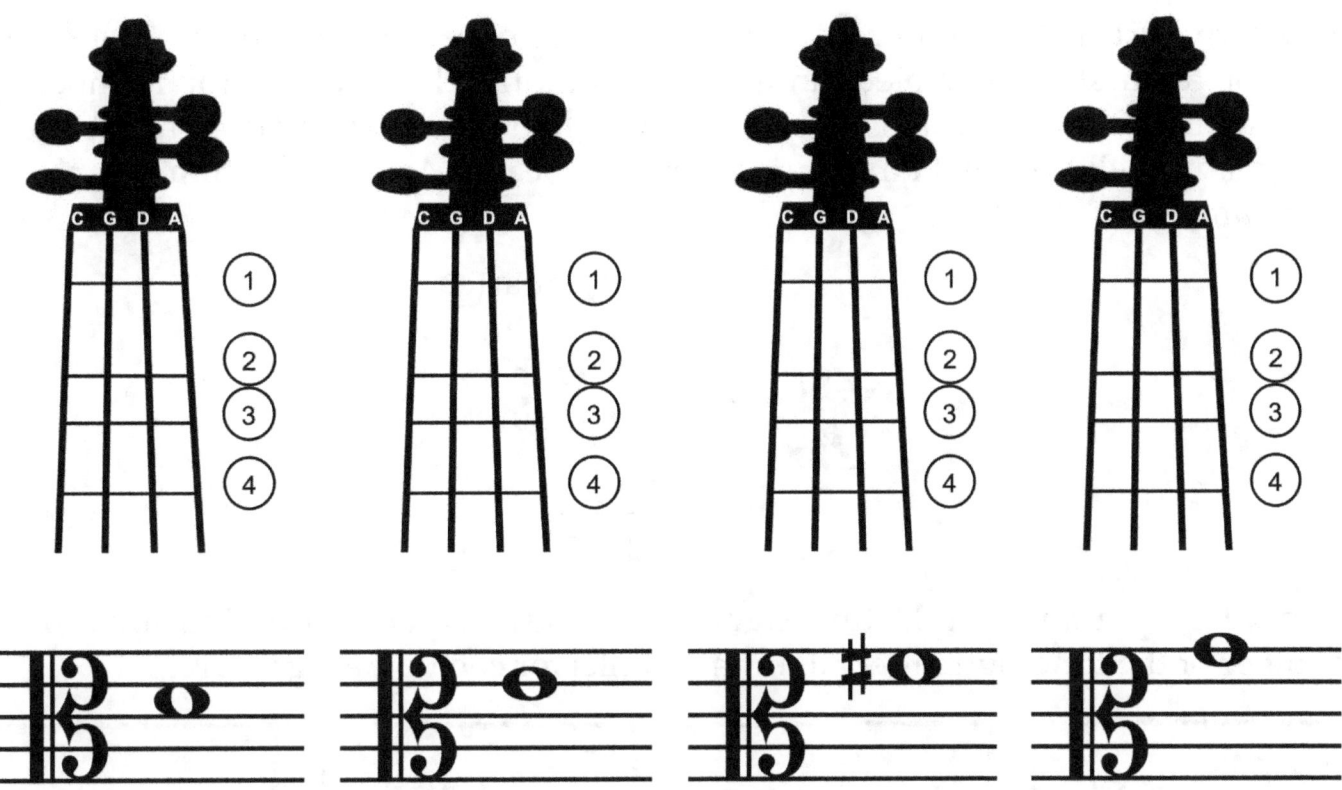

7. Circle the fingerboards whose houses are a half step apart. Draw an X over the fingerboards whose houses are a whole step apart.

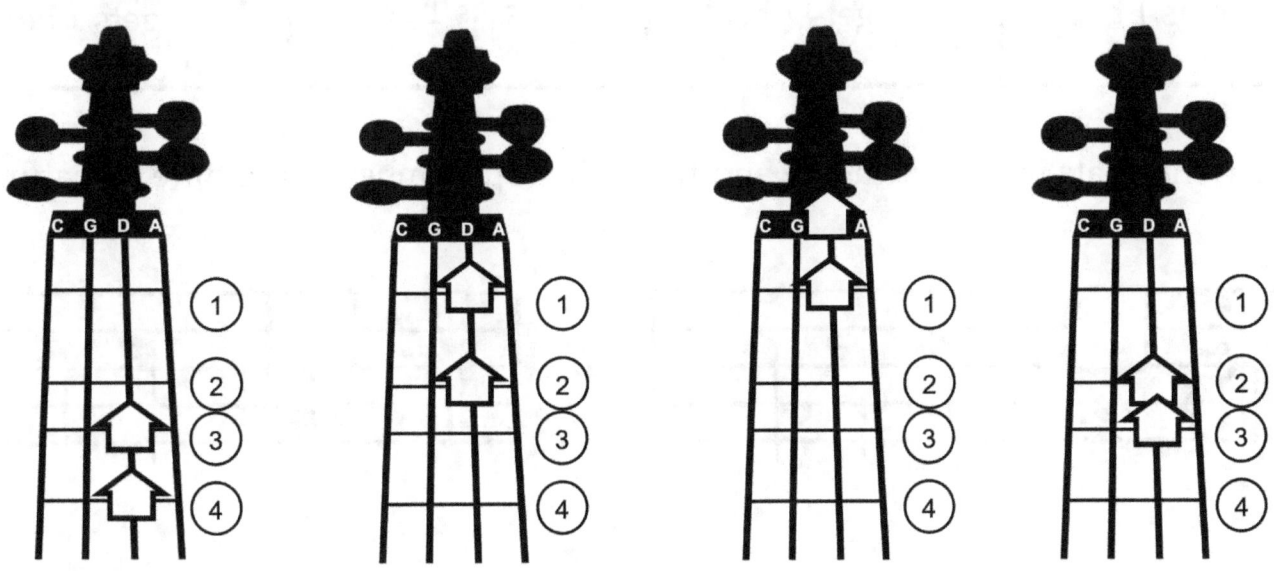

8. On the D string, the half step is between finger numbers _____ and _____.

The letters for these fingers are _____ and _____.

Lesson 21

A **time signature** is the two numbers stacked on top of each other. The time signature is printed on the first line of a piece immediately after the clef sign. The top number of a time signature tells us how many beats are in each measure. The bottom number of the time signature tells us what kind of note gets one beat. A **4 on the bottom means the quarter note gets 1 beat.**

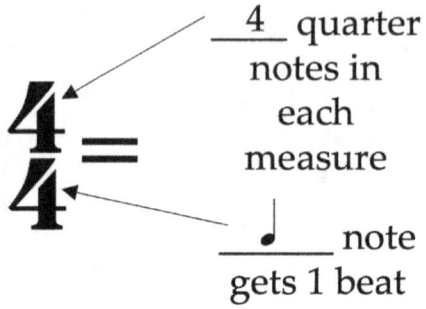

$\dfrac{4}{4}$ = ____4 quarter notes in each measure

____ ♩ note gets 1 beat

1. Circle the top number of the time signatures. Draw a square around the bottom number of the time signature. Fill in the blanks for each time signature.

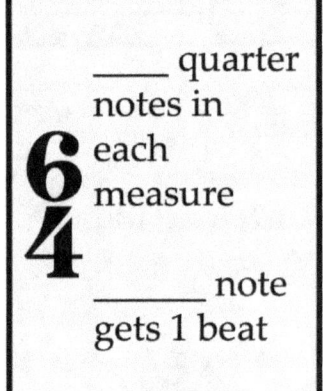

____ quarter notes in each measure

____ note gets 1 beat

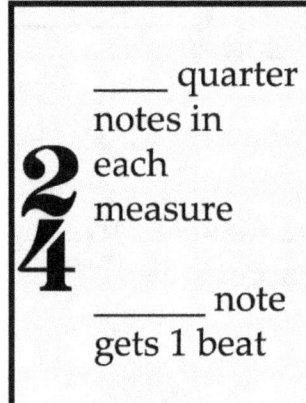

____ quarter notes in each measure

____ note gets 1 beat

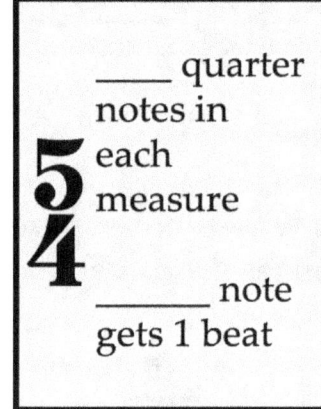

____ quarter notes in each measure

____ note gets 1 beat

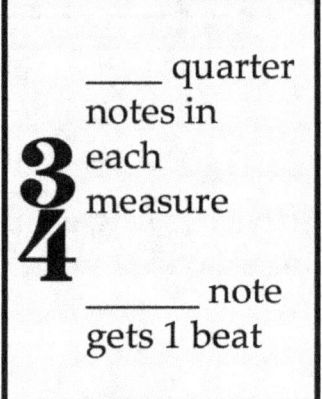

____ quarter notes in each measure

____ note gets 1 beat

2. Count the beats in each measure and fill in the top number of the time signature.

58

3. Write the number of beats for each note in the heart.

Beats:

4. Since the time signature is 4/4 in question 3, there should be a total of 4 beats in each measure. Look at each measure above and add up the number of beats in each measure. Does each measure equal 4 beats? Circle the answer: YES   NO

5. Write the number beats for each note in the heart.

Beats:

6. This time signature is 2/4. There should be a total of 2 beats in each measure. Add up the number of beats in each measure above. Does each measure have 2 beats? Circle the answer: YES   NO

We count the beats in each measure! Each beat gets one number. We start our counting over at the beginning of the next measure. Do you see how each measure has 4 counts? Use your finger and point to each note and say the *counts* out loud.

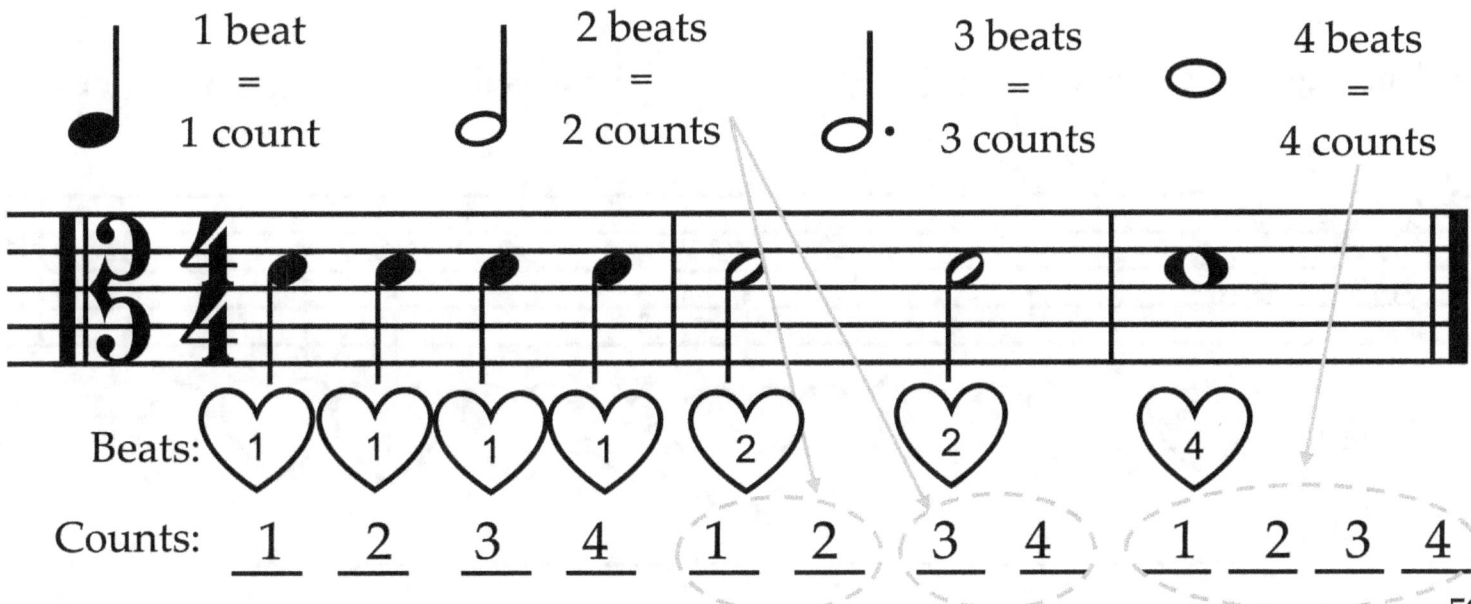

Lesson 22

Fill in the blanks. Then, write the number of beats for each note in the hearts. Write the counts for each measure in the blanks.

1. Time Signature: There are _____ beats in each measure. The _____ gets 1 beat.

Beats:

Counts: __ __ __ __ __ __ __ __ __ __ __ __

2. Time Signature: There are _____ beats in each measure. The _____ gets 1 beat.

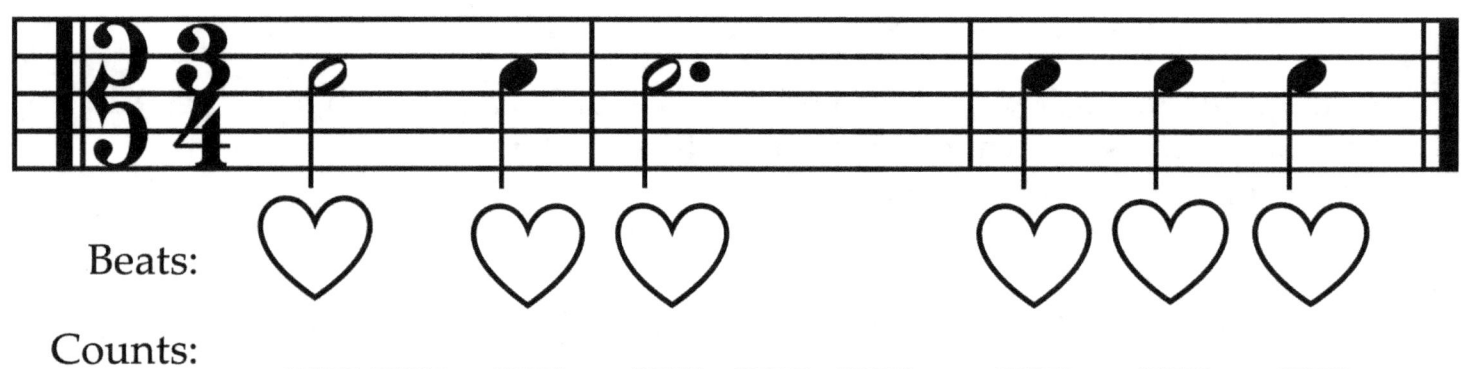

Beats:

Counts: __ __ __ __ __ __ __ __ __

3. Time Signature: There are _____ beats in each measure. The _____ gets 1 beat.

Beats:

Counts: __ __ __ __ __ __ __ __ __ __ __

4. Draw in the missing bar lines. Remember the beats in each measure should add up to the top number of the time signature.

5. Write the top number of the time signature in the box.

61

Lesson 23

To show the notes that are higher or lower than the 5 lines on the staff, we can extend the staff up and down using little lines that look like ladders. These little lines are called **ledger lines**.

1. Draw the ledger line note on the empty staff next to each note.

2. I have 6 quarter notes in each measure. What is my time signature?_____

3. I have 2 quarter notes in each measure. What is my time signature? _____

4. Write the letter names under each note.

5. Draw an alto clef on each empty staff. Then draw a whole note for the letter on the staff.

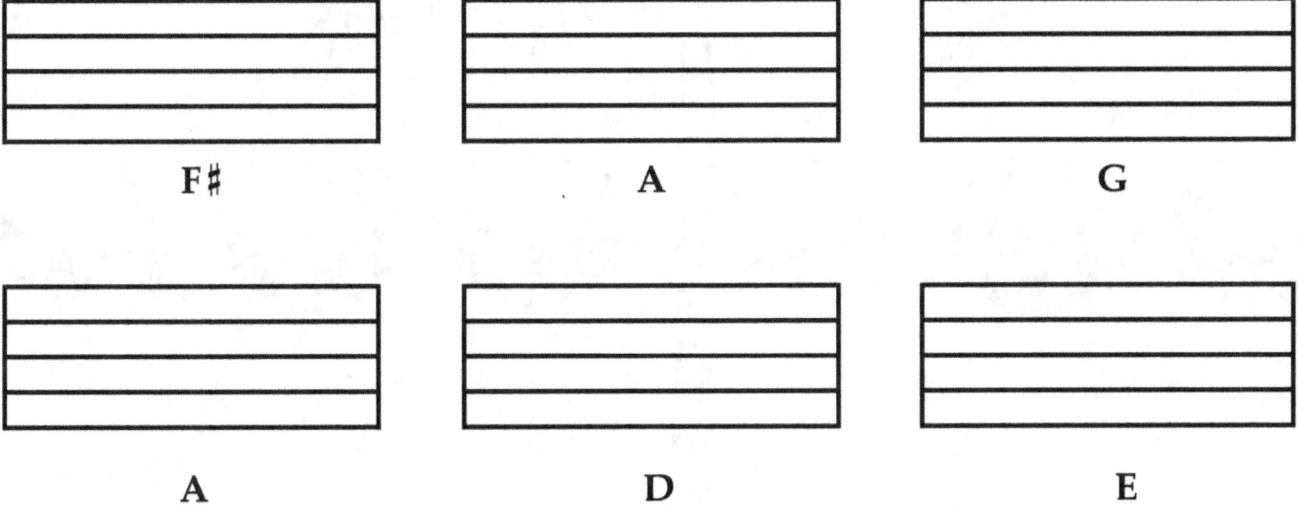

F♯   A   G

A   D   E

6. Write the top number of the time signature in the box.

What do you hear? #6

Place a coin on each coconut. If the notes you hear step up, push a coin up to the top of the tree. If the notes you hear step down, push a coin down to the ground.

1   2   3   4   5   6

Choose from these examples:

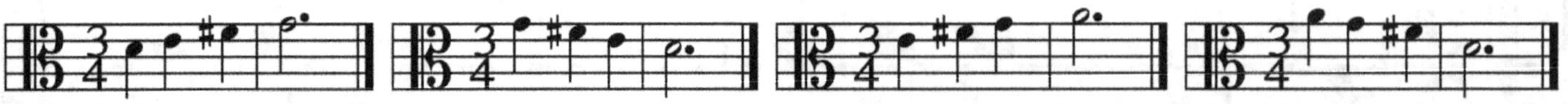

64

Lesson 24

Remember that 4th finger on the D string is A. It is the same note as open A.

Open A is a space note and lives on top of the staff.

1. Trace the alto clef. Draw 3 "A" whole notes on the staff. Write the letter below.

Space on top of the staff
Open A

_____ _____ _____

A (space 4) – step up – land on **B** (ledger line 1).

2. Trace the alto clef. Draw 3 "B" whole notes on the staff. Write the letter below.

Ledger Line 1 = B

_____ _____ _____

Remember!!! Always draw a sharp (♯) on the left side of the note head. It looks like a tic-tac-toe board. Draw the middle square of the sharp on the same line or space as the note.

B (ledger line 1) – step up – land on **C♯** (sits on top of ledger line 1).

3. Trace the alto clef. Draw 3 "C♯" whole notes on the staff. Write the letter below.

Sits on top
of ledger line 1 = C♯

_____ _____ _____

65

C♯(space above ledger line 1) – step up – land on **D** (ledger line 2).

4. Trace the alto clef. Draw 2 leger lines and 3 "D" whole notes on ledger line 2. Write the letter below.

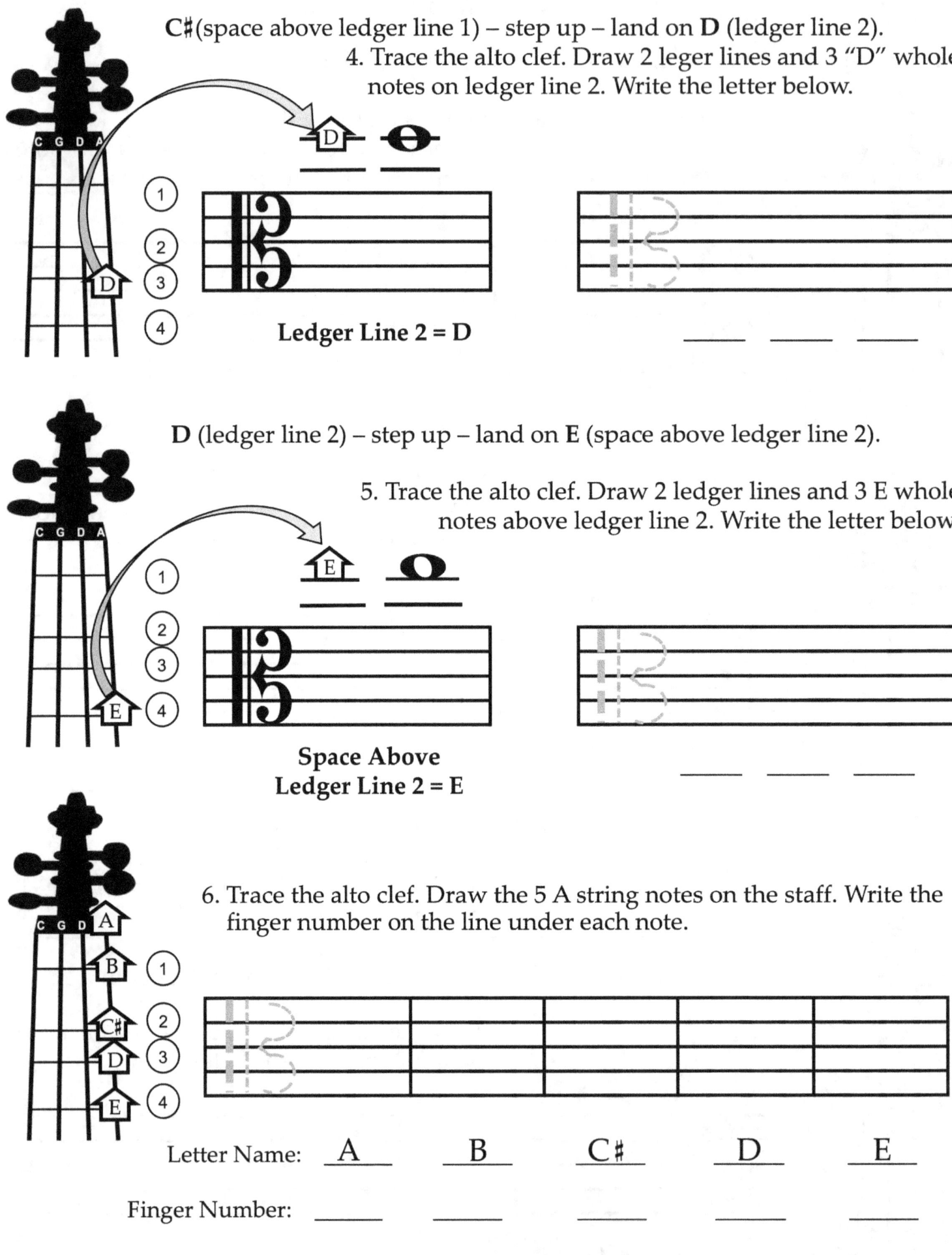

Ledger Line 2 = D

_____ _____ _____

D (ledger line 2) – step up – land on **E** (space above ledger line 2).

5. Trace the alto clef. Draw 2 ledger lines and 3 E whole notes above ledger line 2. Write the letter below.

**Space Above
Ledger Line 2 = E**

_____ _____ _____

6. Trace the alto clef. Draw the 5 A string notes on the staff. Write the finger number on the line under each note.

Letter Name: __A__   __B__   __C♯__   __D__   __E__

Finger Number: _____   _____   _____   _____

Discover the Composers

7. Fill in the letter of the note to learn about the life of a great composer.

G___orge Fre___eri___ H___n___el w___s ___orn in

G___rm___ny in 1685. H___ pl___y___ ___ ___oth

violin ___n___ org___n. He ___ompos___ ___ music for

the King of ___ngl___n___. He wrote one pi___ ___ ___

for the or___h___str___ to play from a ___ ___rg___ on the

riv___r. He ___ ___lle___ it "W___t___r musi___."

8. Name a piece you have played by this composer:_____

67

9. Color by Note: Color the treble clef and notes as you listen to George Fredric Handel's Sonata in E Major, Op. 1, No. 6, I. Allegro.

Color Code:
Open A – Red
B – Green
C# – Yellow
D – Purple
E – Orange

Lesson 25

1. Write in the letters for each A string house.

2. Write the finger in each circle.

3. Fill in the blanks under each note.

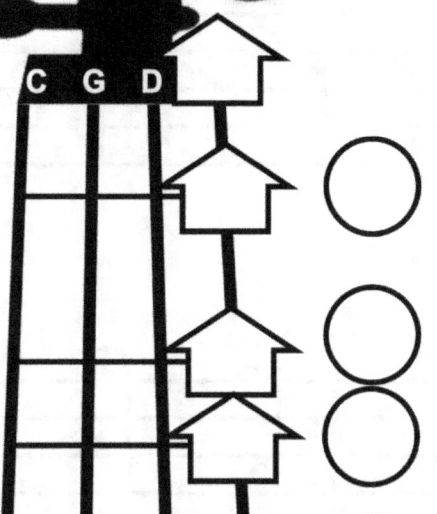

Letter _____

Finger Number _____

Letter _____

Finger Number _____

Letter _____

Finger Number _____

Letter _____

Finger Number _____

Letter _____

Finger Number _____

True   or   False   4. A ledger line extends the staff up or down.

True   or   False   5. On the A string, B up to C♯ is a half step.

True   or   False   6. On the A string, C♯ up to D is a half step.

7. Draw in the missing bar lines.

8. Write the time signature at the beginning of each staff.

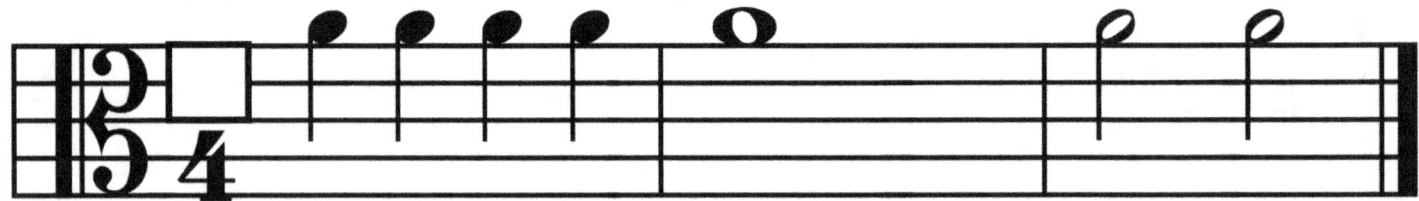

9. Write the number of beats each note gets in the hearts. Write the counts for each measure in the blanks.

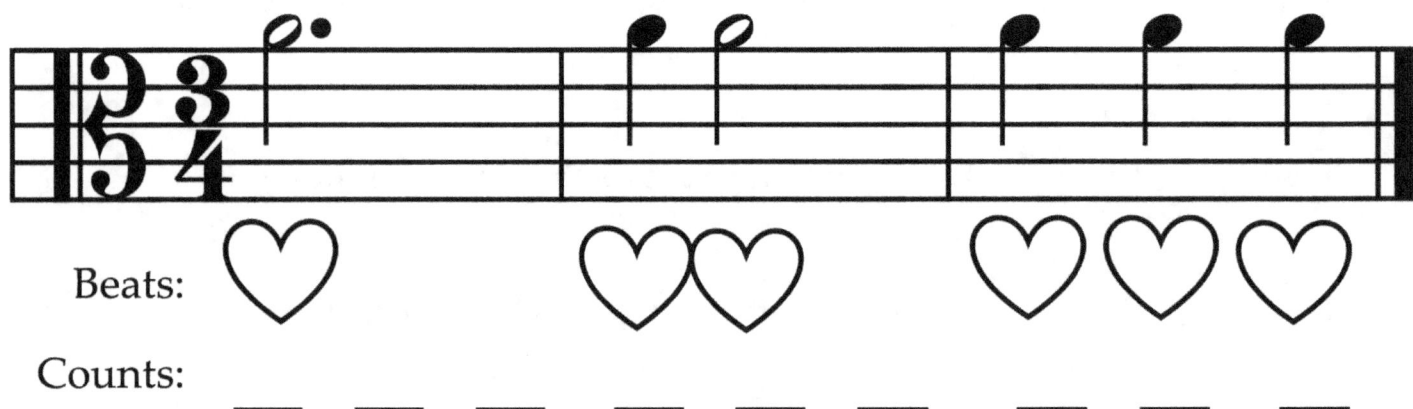

Beats:

Counts: ___ ___ ___ ___ ___ ___ ___

10. Color by Note: Color the picture below following the color code for the the D and A string notes. Listen to "Water Droplets" by a composer from Finland, Jean Sibelius.

Color Key
Open D – Red
E – Green
F♯ – Purple
G – Blue
A – Yellow
B – Teal
C♯ – Orange
High D – Pink
High E – Gray

Did you know?
When we plucks the strings, it is called **pizzicato** [pits-ih-ca-toe], or *pizz.* [pits] for short. When we play with the bow it is called **arco** [ahr-co]. "Water Droplets" is all pizzicato!

Lesson 26

1. Draw a line to the correct part of the bow.

screw   frog   grip   wrapping   stick   horsehair   tip

Bowing Symbols

Tone is the sound that the viola makes when it plays. How each note starts and ends is called **articulation.** For stringed instruments, the bow does most of the articulation work. **Detaché** [day-ta-shay] means separated. Detaché is the basic bow stroke we use to play our instrument. In the detaché bow stroke, the bow alternates between down bows and up bows. Sometimes we refer to this as "separate bows."

◼ This symbol means to use a down bow. A down bow pulls the bow from frog to toward the tip.

V This symbol means to use an up bow. An up bow pushes the bow from tip to toward the frog.

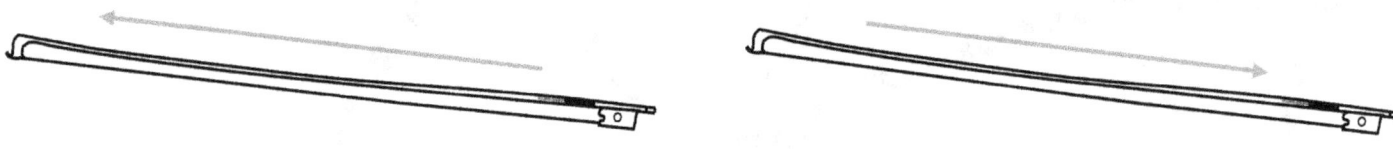

2. *Twinkle, Twinkle Little Star* begins with a _____ (draw the bow mark) and uses detaché bow strokes.

3. Practice drawing the down bow and up bow symbols by write the correct bow symbol above each note. The first one is done for you.

You should NOT write a bow symbol above every note in your music. This exercise is only practice for writing bow markings. The first note of a piece will usually have a bowing symbol telling you how to begin. Bow marks are only written over a few notes in a piece. If there is no bow marking, play detaché bows. If there is a change in the down up pattern, a bow marking will be added.

4. Circle whether the action in the picture is moving up or down.

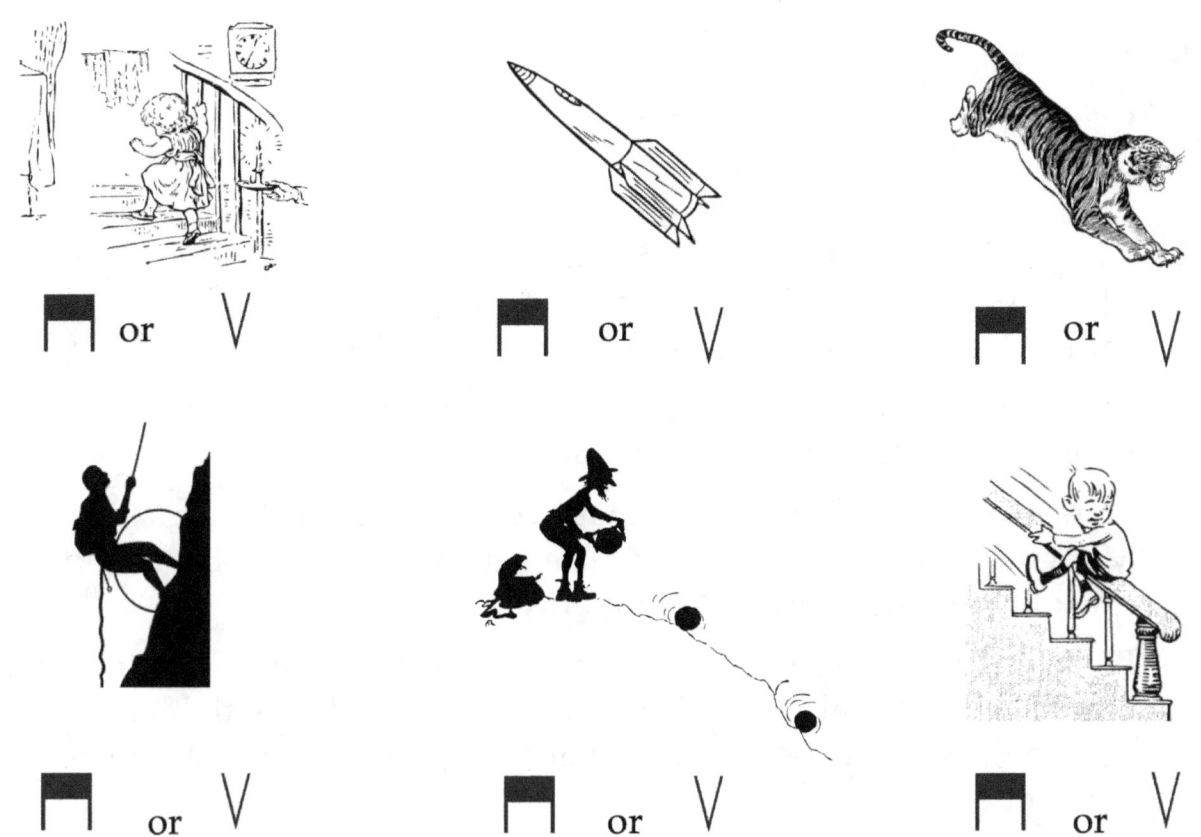

5. In each box fill in what bow direction the bow is playing.

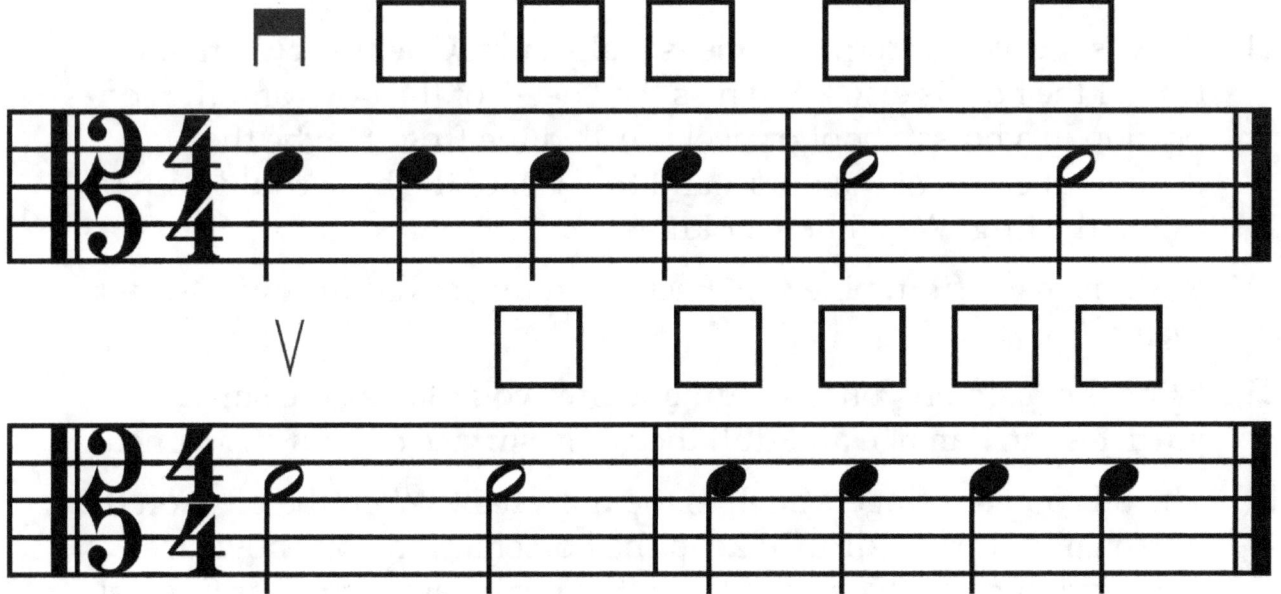

6. Write the term next to the definition. (*articulation, detaché, tone*)

_____ - the sound that the viola makes when it plays.

_____ - how a note starts or ends.

_____ - separate bows.

?? *Did you know?*

- ❑ Did you know that bows used to look like this? The stick of the bow curved up, rather than down like the modern bow.

- ❑ There are about 150 horsehairs on a violin bow, and about 200 horsehairs on a cello bow.

- ❑ Horsehair comes from horses that live in very cold climates like Mongolia, Siberia, and Canada. The hair they grow is strong and thick. It's just what is needed for bow hair.

- ❑ Bleaching horsehair weakens it so bow hair comes from white horses that have white hair. Some bass players like to play with black horsehair. Black horsehair is thicker and grips the thick strings of a bass better.

- ❑ Bow makers clean and sort the horsehair. They call this "dressing" the hair. In dressing the hair, they discard hairs that are not perfect or that are too short.

- ❑ Why is it called a frog? No one is really sure. One theory is that the frog of the bow is also known as the "heel" of the bow, and the soft portion in a horse's hoof or heel is called the frog. Maybe they decided the heel of the horse, and the heel of the bow could both be called the frog. We will never know!

- ❑ Rosin is made from pine sap. Each rosin maker has his own "secret recipe."

- ❑ Wipe the rosin off your instrument after you play as the small particles can damage and dull the shiny surface of your instrument.

- ❑ The oils on your fingers stick to the horsehair. When the oil is on the horsehair it attracts dirt. To keep the horsehair on your bow clean and working well. Do not to touch the horsehair with your fingers!

Music Note Bowling

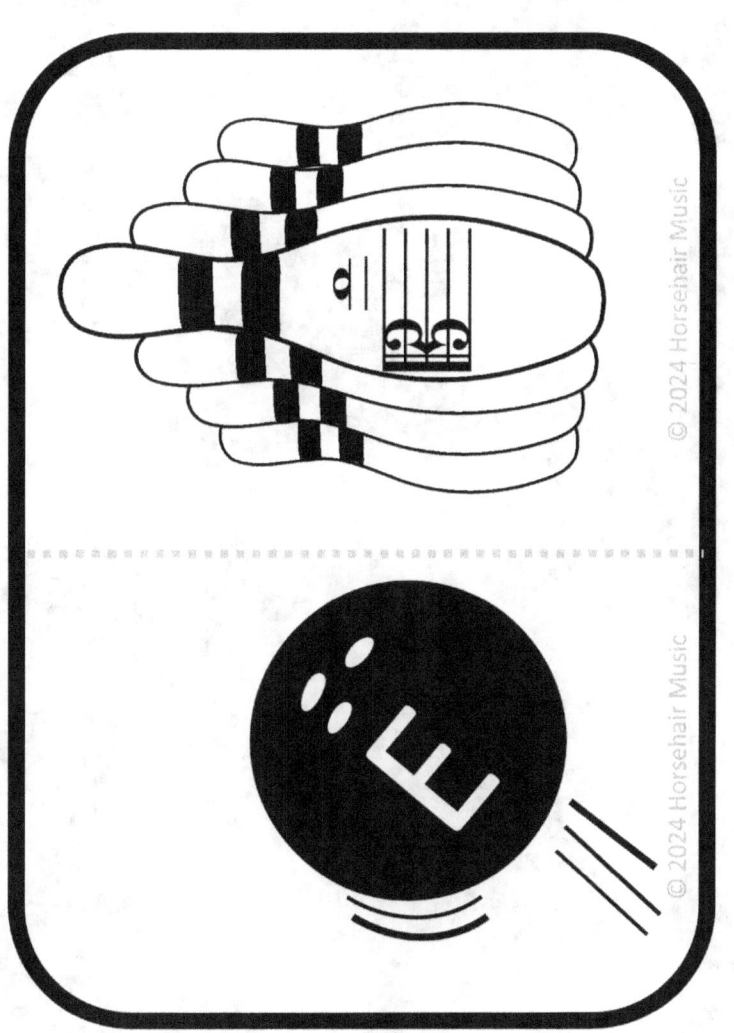

Preparing to play:
1. Cut out each card and cut down the center on the dotted line.
2. Group the cards with staff notes in one pile, and the cards with bowling balls in another pile.
3. Take the staff note cards and spread them out face down.
4. Take the bowling ball cards and spread them out face down.

How to play with one player:
1. Turn one card over in each group. If the letter on the bowling ball does not match the staff note, turn both cards back over, face down.
2. Continue turning one card over in each group until you find a match.
3. Your goal is to match all the staff cards to the correct letter on the bowling ball card.

How to play with two or more players:
1. The first player turns over one bowling ball card and one staff card. If the cards match, that player takes both the cards and sets them aside. If the cards do not match, the player turns both cards over.
2. If the player has a match, he takes another turn. If the player does not have a match, the next player takes a turn looking to find a match.
3. Continue until all the cards in both piles have been matched.

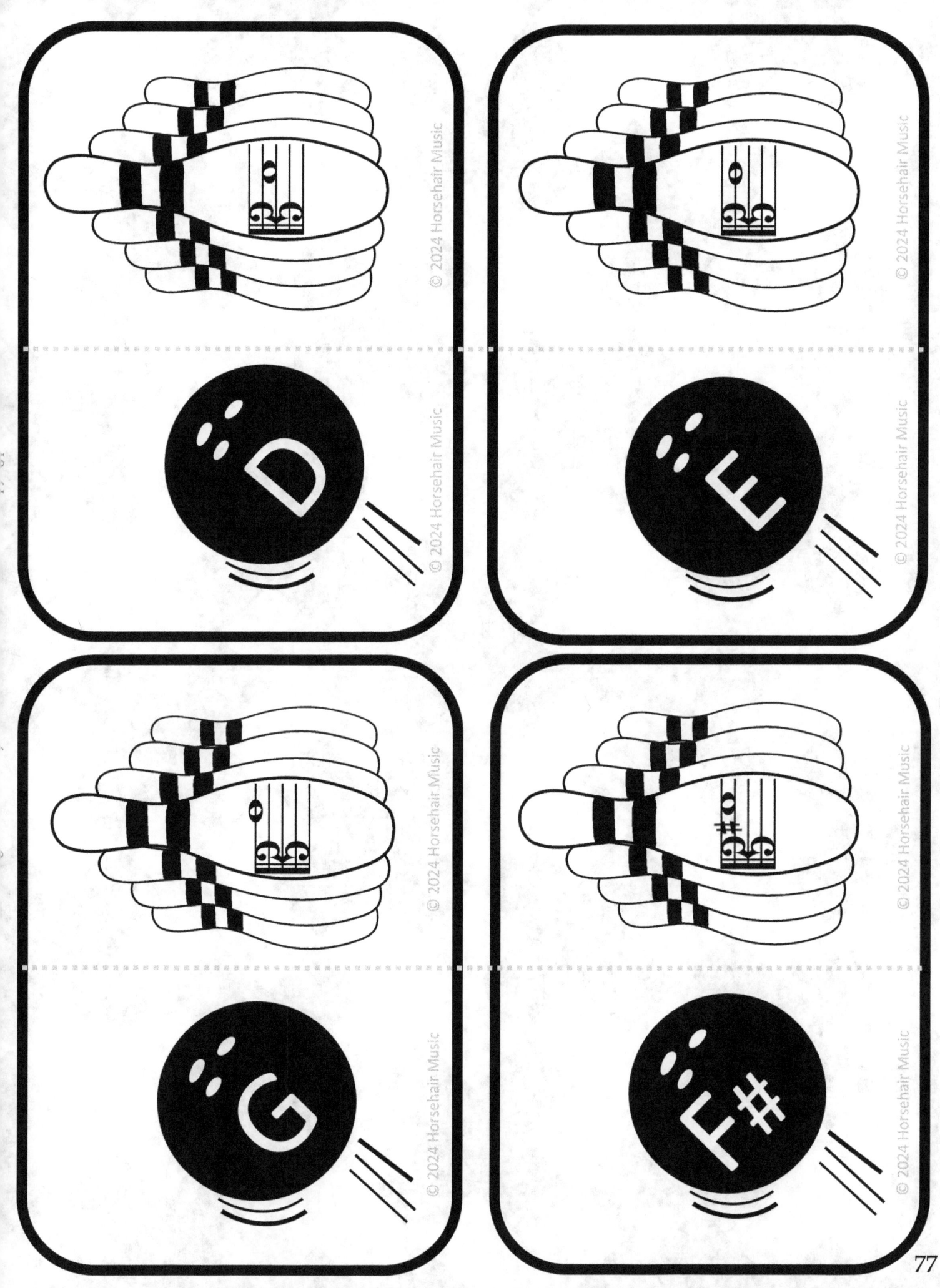

© 2024 Horsehair Music

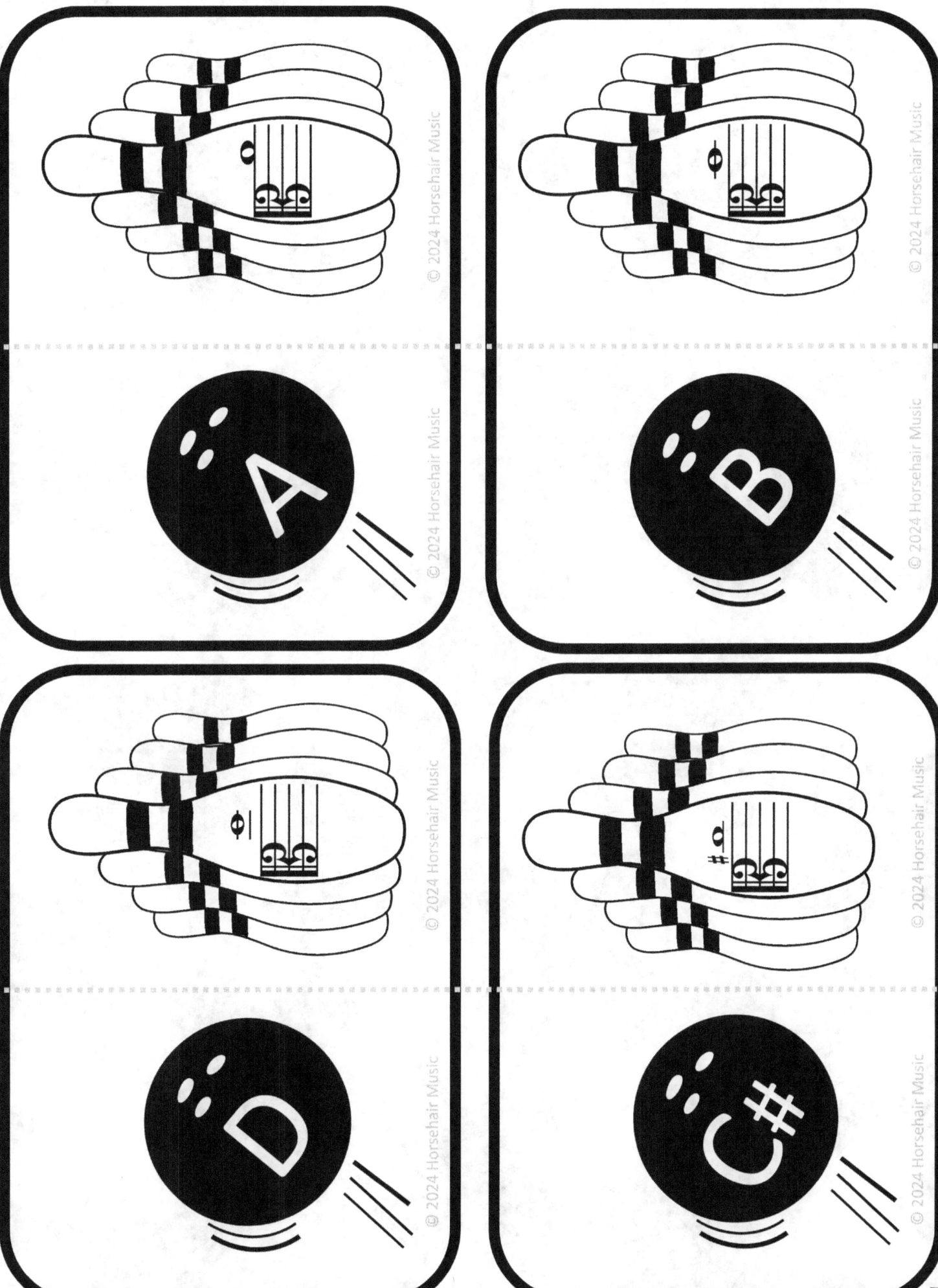

© 2024 Horsehair Music

Lesson 27

1. Draw a line matching the fingerboard house to the staff note.

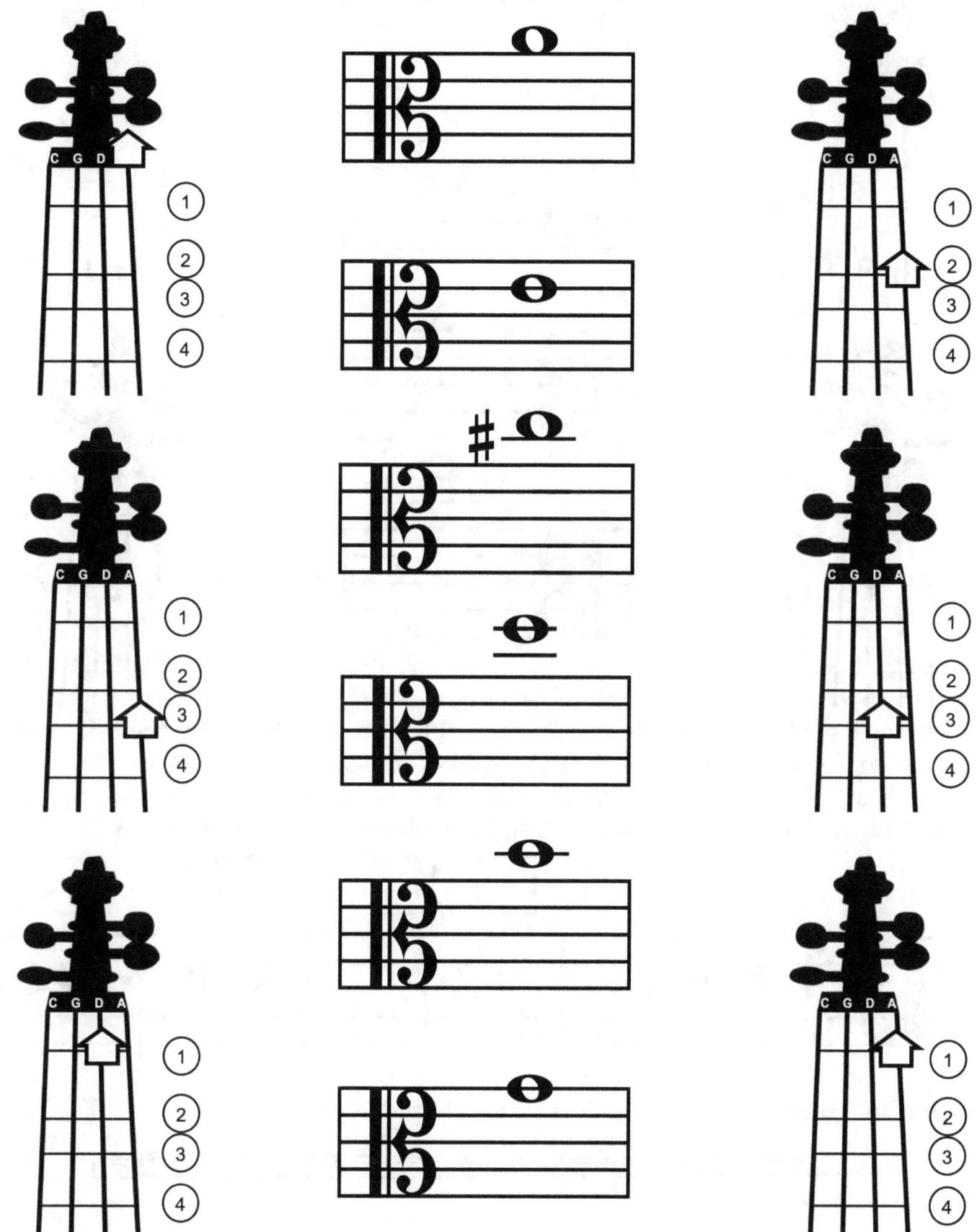

2. Draw a line matching the fingerboard to the staff note.

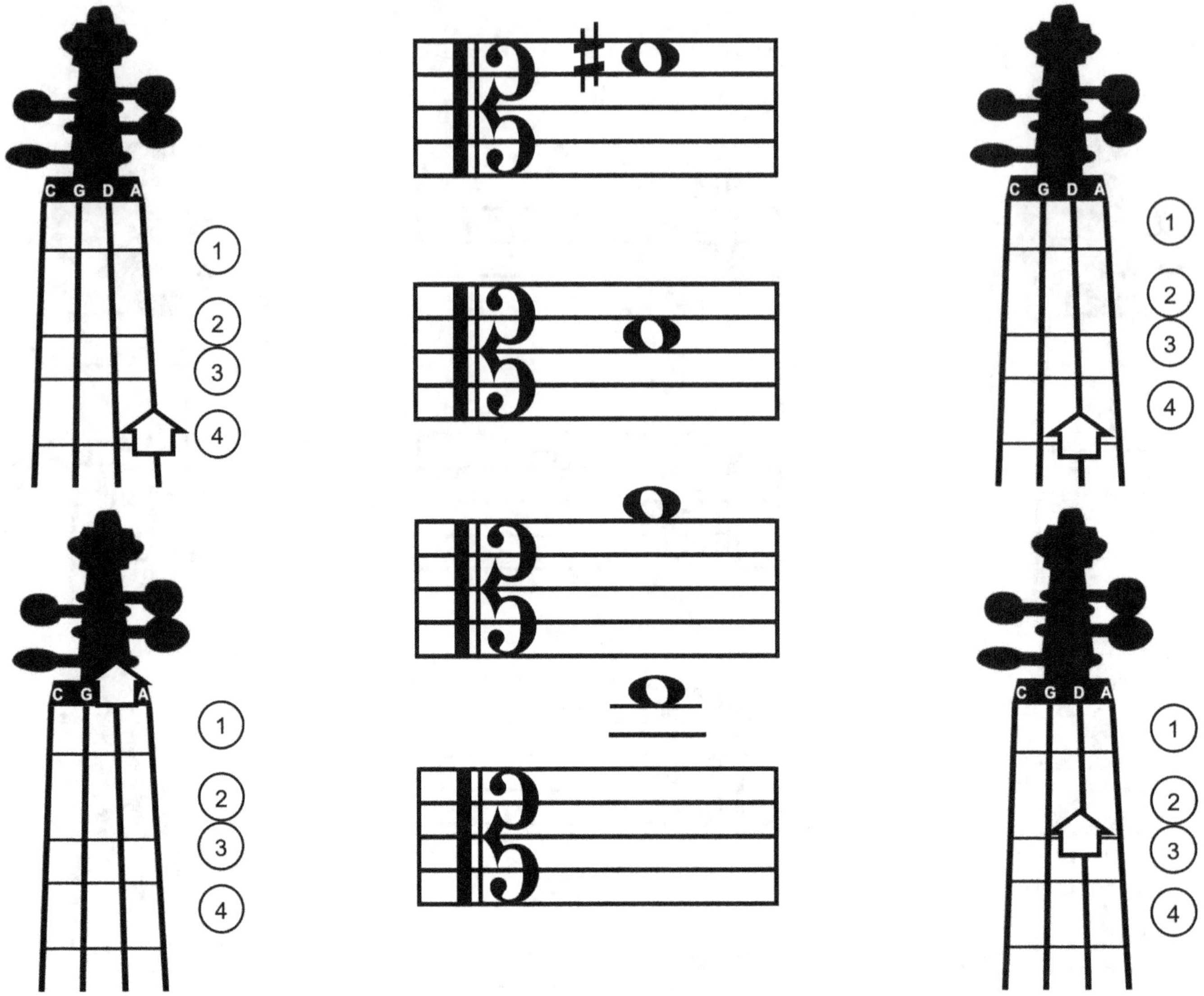

3. To know what bow direction to use for each note, put your finger on the first note say, "down." Then move your finger to the next note and say, "up." Move to the next note and say, "down." Move from one note to the next, switch between saying "down" or "up" for each note. If there is a box, write the bow direction in that box

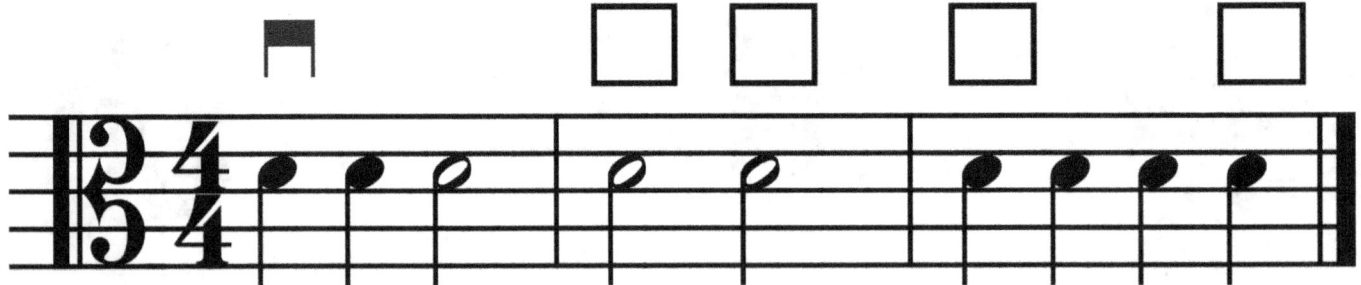

4. Draw a line from the term to the correct part of the bow.

　　tip　frog　stick　wrapping　horsehair　grip　screw

5. Draw an alto clef on each empty staff. Draw a whole note on the correct place on the staff.

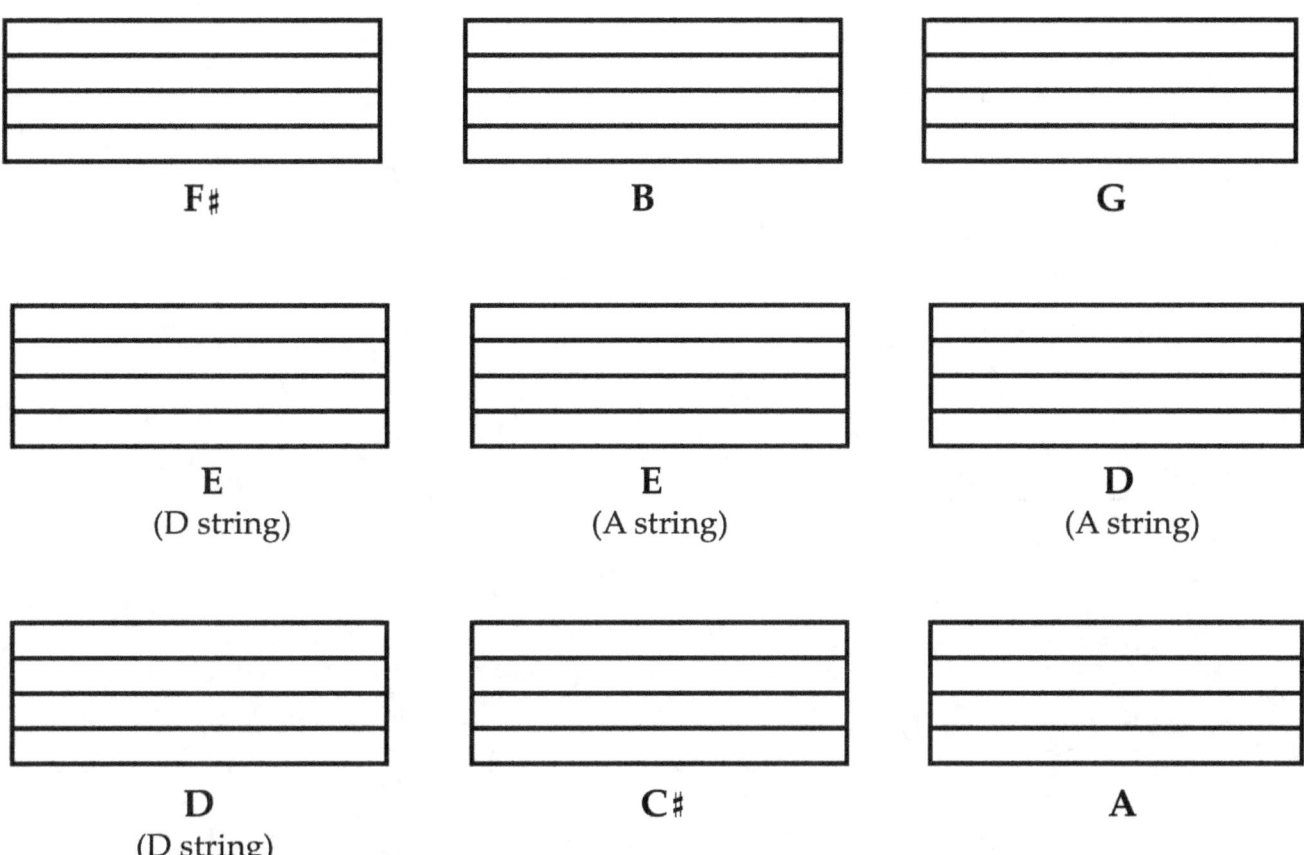

F♯

B

G

E
(D string)

E
(A string)

D
(A string)

D
(D string)

C♯

A

6. Draw the bar lines on the staff.

Lesson 28

Match the symbol or definition to the word.

1. _____	Whole Note	A.	f
2. _____	Dotted Half Note	B.	p
3. _____	Half Note	C.	(half note with stem down)
4. _____	Quarter Note	D.	(dotted half note)
5. _____	Adagio	E.	(whole note)
6. _____	Allegro	F.	(quarter note)
7. _____	Forte	G.	(double bar line)
8. _____	Piano	H.	(down bow symbol)
9. _____	Down Bow	I.	V
10. _____	Up Bow	J.	(bass clef)
11. _____	Double Bar Line	K.	(treble clef)
12. _____	Alto Clef	L.	(alto clef)
13. _____	Treble Clef	M.	Fast and Lively
14. _____	Bass Clef	N.	Slow

15. Write the number of beats each note gets in the hearts. Write the counts for each measure on the lines.

Beats: ♡ ♡ ♡ ♡ ♡ ♡

Counts: ___ ___ ___ ___ ___ ___ ___ ___ ___ ___

16. To discover the hidden picture color all the boxes that have a note.

𝄞	▬	*p*	♩	♩	*mp*	𝄁	𝄞	4/4
▬	♩	♩	𝄡	𝄇	𝅝	▬	𝄽	♩
3/4	𝅝	♩.	𝄢	▬	𝄁	♩	𝄡	𝄽
mf	𝄢	4/4	2/4	*p*	♩	𝄡	♯	♩
▬	♯	𝄽	3/4	♩	▬	*f*	𝄽	*mf*
p	𝄁	𝄽	♩.	𝄞	▬	2/4	𝄢	▬
▬	3/4	𝅝	𝄆	*mp*	▬	4/4	𝄆	*mp*

17. What music symbol did you discover? _____

18. _____ read music in this clef.
    (instrument)

20. True   or   False   A symphony orchestra has only stringed instruments. (p.7)

20. True   or   False   A string orchestra has only stringed instruments.

85

Lesson 29

1. Write the letter name under each note and discover a word.

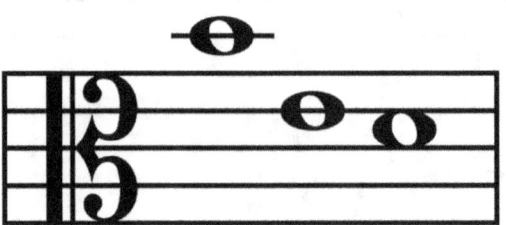

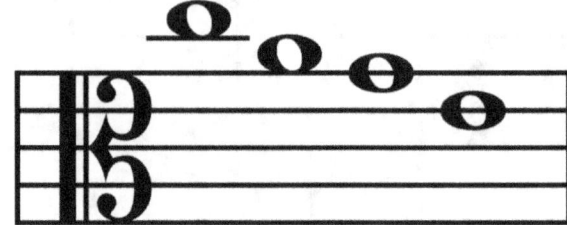

____ ___

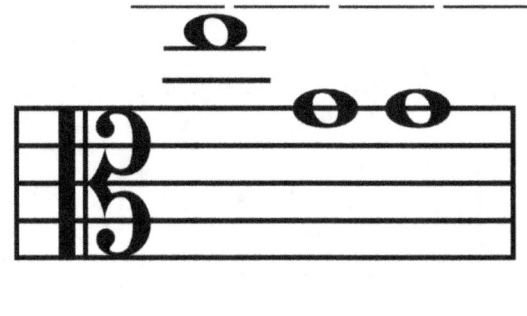

____ ____ ____ ____

____ ____ ____

2. Draw the bowing symbol.

Down Bow = _____ Up Bow = _____

3. Write one letter of the music alphabet in each octagon starting on D.

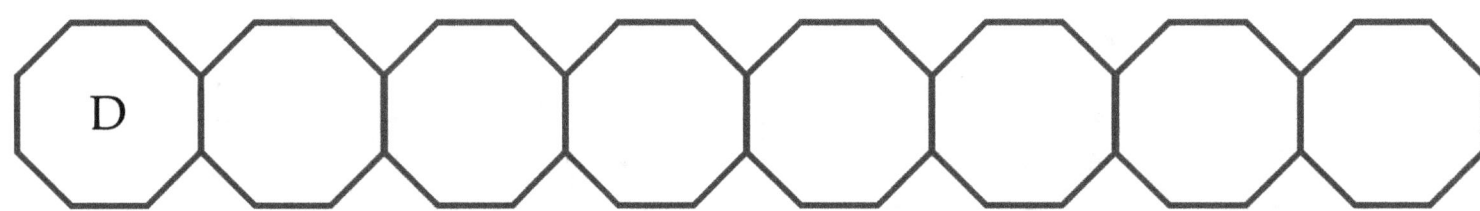

4. Circle if the notes are stepping up, stepping down, or repeating.

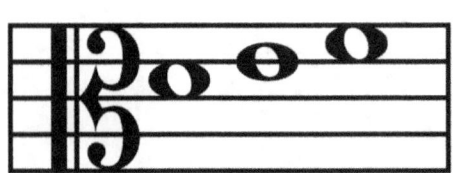

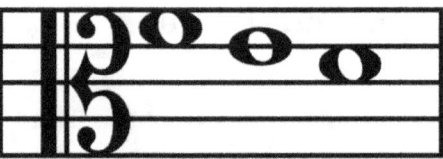

Step Up   Step Down   Step Up   Step Down   Step Up   Step Down

Repeat   Repeat   Repeat

5. Write the number of beats each note receives in the hearts. Write the counts for each measure in the blanks.

Beats:

Counts: ___ ___ ___ ___ ___ ___

Beats:

Counts: ___ ___ ___ ___ ___ ___

6. Write the letter names under each note.

___ ___ ___ ___

___ ___ ___ ___

___ ___ ___ ___

Lesson 30

1. Write the letter name in each house on the D string and A string.

2. Write the finger numbers in each circle.

3. Draw an alto clef.

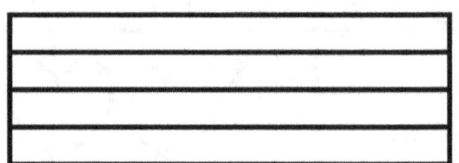

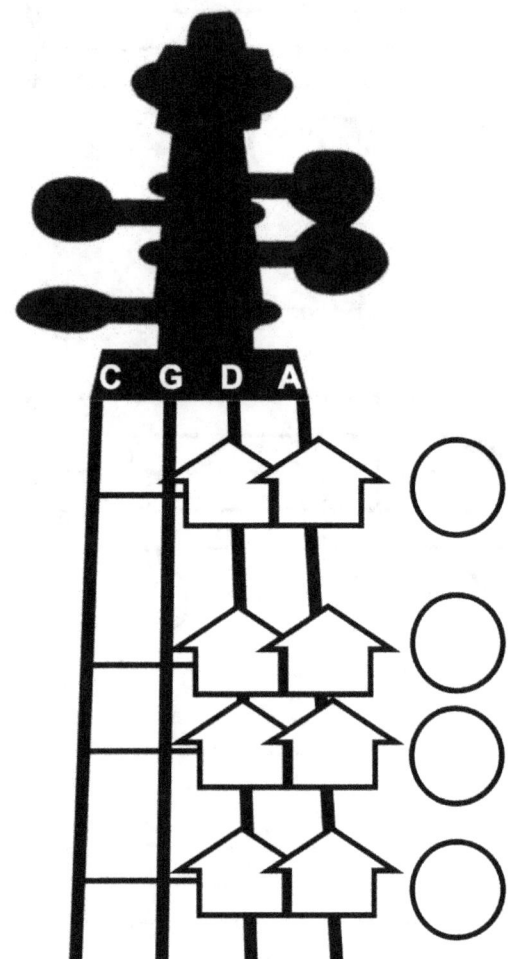

4. Color the houses that are a half step apart purple on the D string and A string.

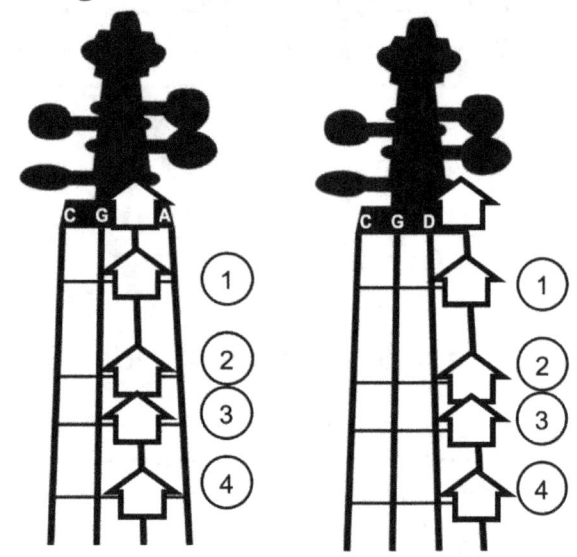

5. Fill in the blanks.

A _____ _____ means your fingers are close together. (p. 44)

A _____ _____ is when there is space between your fingers. (p. 44)

Treble	Bass	Alto	6. Means high. (p. 30)
Treble	Bass	Alto	7. Means low.
Treble	Bass	Alto	8. Violinists read notes in this clef.
Treble	Bass	Alto	9. Double Bassists read notes in this clef.
Treble	Bass	Alto	10. Violists read notes in this clef.

11. Draw an alto clef on each empty staff. Draw a whole note on the correct place on the staff.

C#

E
(D string)

G

F

A

B

D
(D string)

D
(A String)

E
(A String)

12. Write the letter for each note in the blank.

13. Draw two more whole notes.

Stepping Down

Repeating

Stepping Up

Bonus: Unscramble the letters. What word do the letters spell?

_____

89

Glossary

Adagio – [tempo] Italian word meaning slow. (p. 26)

Allegro – [tempo] Italian word meaning fast, happy with energy. (p. 26)

Alto Clef – Violas read music using the alto clef. Sometimes called the C clef because the clef points to C line on the staff. (p. 30)

Andante – [tempo] Italian word meaning walking speed. (p. 26)

Arco – Italian word meaning play with the bow. (p.71)

Articulation – How a note begins and/or ends. (p. 70)

Bar Line – A vertical line that touches lines 1 and 5 to create measures. (p. 56)

Bass Clef – Cellos and basses read music using the bass clef. Sometimes called the F clef because the clef points to F line on the staff. (p. 30)

Detaché – [bowing] French word meaning detached. Each note is played with a separate bow stroke. (p. 70)

Dotted Half Note – Gets 3 beats in 4/4 time. (p. 23)

Double Bar Line – A thin line by a thick line. Signals the end of the piece. (p. 56)

Down Bow – [bowing] Moving the bow from frog toward the tip. (p. 70)

Dynamics – Volume; how loud or soft to play notes. (p. 10, 21)

Forte – [dynamic] Italian word meaning loud. (p. 21, 34)

Half Note – Gets 2 beats in 4/4 time. (p. 20)

Half Step – closest distance between two notes; fingers are close together on the fingerboard. (p. 44, 48)

Harmony – When two or more notes sound together at the same time. (p. 10)

Ledger Line – A small line that extends the staff. It can be above or below the 5 staff lines. (p. 62)

Measure – The space in between bar lines. (p. 56)

Music Alphabet – First seven letters of the English alphabet. (p. 10, 22)

Note Head – The round part of a note. (p. 19)

Open String – Playing a string without fingers. (p. 11)

Piano – [dynamic] Italian word meaning soft. (p. 21, 34)

Pitch – the sound of each note. (p. 10)

Pizzicato – Italian word meaning pluck the string. Abbreviated *pizz*. (p. 71)

Quarter Note – Gets 1 beat in 4/4 time. (p. 19)

Rhythm – How long or short a pitch is held. (p. 10, 19)

Staff – 5 lines and 4 spaces that show pitches. (p. 28)

Stem – The line that goes up on the right or down on the left side of a note head. (p. 19)

Step – The letter before or after a letter in the music alphabet. The line or space above or below a note on the staff. The finger number before or after a finger on the fingerboard. (p. 37, 39, 41, 44, 45, 48)

String Orchestra – A group of musicians who only play stringed instruments. (p. 7)

Symphony Orchestra – A group of musicians who play woodwind, brass, percussion, and string instruments. (p. 7)

Tempo – Speed, how fast or slow music is played. (p. 26)

Time Signature – Found at the beginning of a piece. Top number tells the number of beats in each measure. The bottom number tells what kind of note gets 1 beat. A 4 on the bottom means the quarter note gets one beat. (p. 58)

Treble Clef – Violins read music using the treble clef. Sometimes called the G clef because the clef points to G line on the staff. (p. 30, 32)

Up Bow – Moving the bow from the tip toward the frog. (p. 70)

Whole Note – Gets 4 beats in 4/4 time. (p. 24)

Whole Step – 2 half steps together. Space between fingers on the fingerboard. (p. 44, 48)

Extra Ear Training Practice A: High or Low & Open Strings

If you hear high notes, color the bird. If you hear low notes, color the worm.

1	2	3

If you hear high notes, color the cloud. If you hear low notes, color the flowers.

4	5	6

Color the house of the open string that you hear.

7.    8.    9.

Choose from these examples:

For questions 7-9 play a rhythm pattern on an open string.

92

Extra Ear Training Practice B: Loud or Soft & Open Strings

If you hear loud, color the roaring hippo. If you hear soft notes, color the frog.

1

2

3

If you hear loud notes, color the boy yelling. If you hear soft notes, color the girl reading.

4

5

6

Color the house of the open string that you hear.

7.

8.

9.

The teacher may choose from these examples and add a dynamic *f* or *p*. For questions 7-9, choose a rhythm pattern to play on an open string.

Extra Ear Training Practice C: Long and Short Patterns

You will hear several notes for each box. When you hear a long note, draw a line. When you hear a short note, draw a dot. Draw all of the notes that you hear in the order that you hear them.

1.

2.

3.

4.

Choose from these examples:

Extra Ear Training Practice D: Adagio or Allegro

If the music you hear is slow, circle Adagio. If the music you hear is fast, circle Allegro.

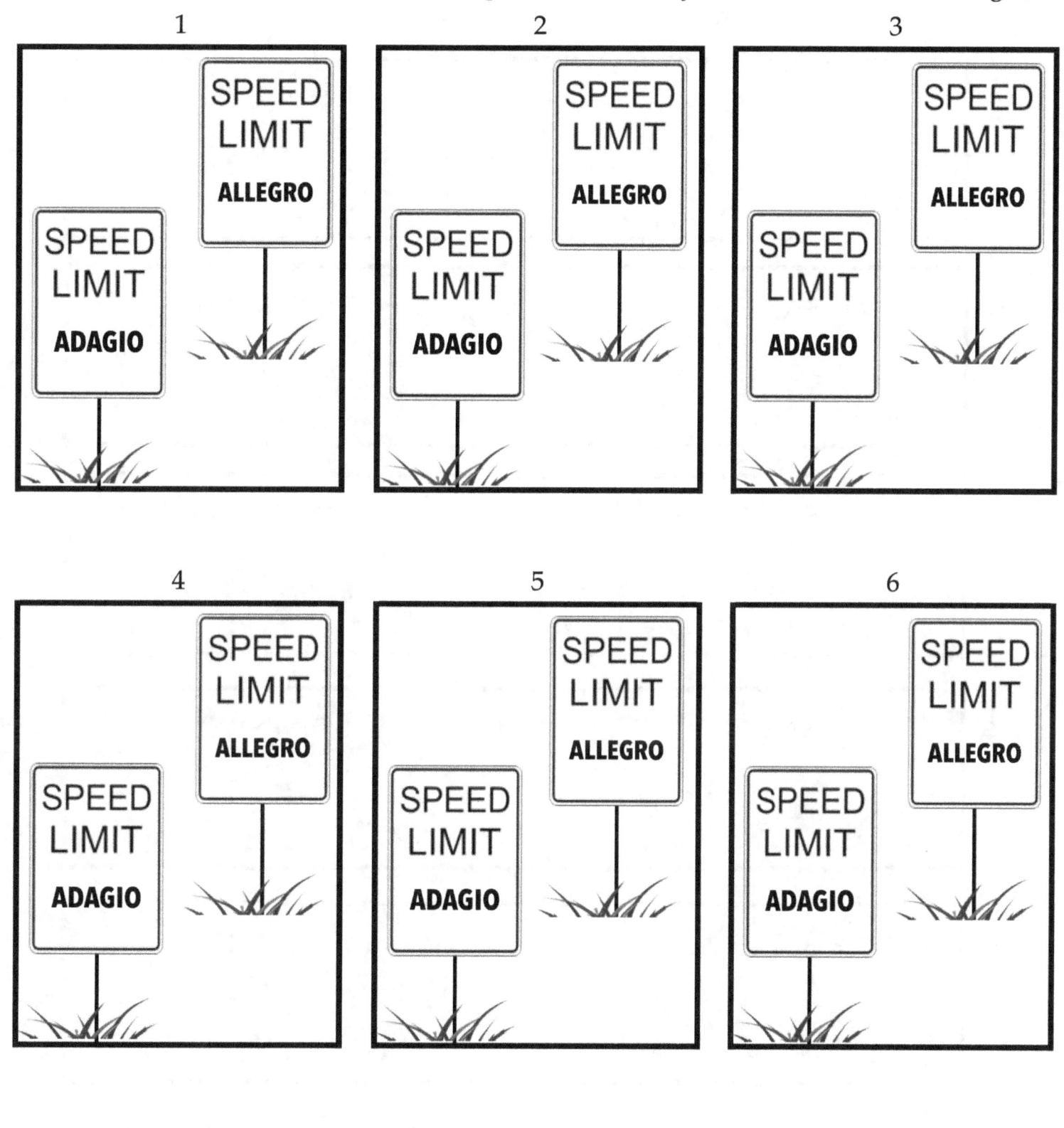

Choose from these examples and play it fast or slow.

Extra Ear Training Practice E: Same or Different

If you hear the same note 3 times, circle the cupcakes that are the same. If you hear 3 notes that are different, circle the cupcakes that are different.

1.　　SAME　　　　　　　　　　DIFFERENT

2.　　SAME　　　　　　　　　　DIFFERENT

3.　　SAME　　　　　　　　　　DIFFERENT

4.　　SAME　　　　　　　　　　DIFFERENT

5.　　SAME　　　　　　　　　　DIFFERENT

Choose from these examples.

Extra Ear Training Practice F: Forte or Piano

Circle the dynamic you hear. If the music you hear is loud, circle *f* for forte. If the music you hear is soft, circle *p* for piano.

1.

f or p

2.

f or p

3.

f or p

4.

f or p

5.

f or p

Choose from these examples:

Hooray!

_____

has completed
The Magic of Music Theory
Primer
and is now ready for Book 1

_____
(Teacher)

_____
(Date)

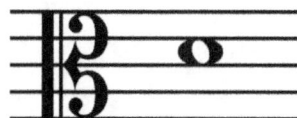

© 2024 Horsehair Music. The Magic of Music Theory Primer

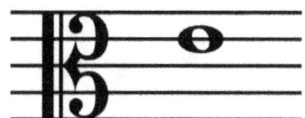

© 2024 Horsehair Music. The Magic of Music Theory Primer

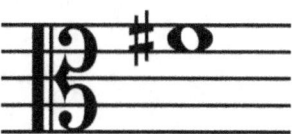

© 2024 Horsehair Music. The Magic of Music Theory Primer

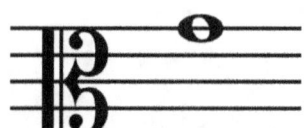

© 2024 Horsehair Music. The Magic of Music Theory Primer

© 2024 Horsehair Music. The Magic of Music Theory Primer

© 2024 Horsehair Music. The Magic of Music Theory Primer

© 2024 Horsehair Music. The Magic of Music Theory Primer

© 2024 Horsehair Music. The Magic of Music Theory Primer

© 2024 Horsehair Music. The Magic of Music Theory Primer

F#

2nd finger on D

© 2024 Horsehair Music. The Magic of Music Theory Primer

E

1st finger on D

© 2024 Horsehair Music. The Magic of Music Theory Primer

D

Open D

© 2024 Horsehair Music. The Magic of Music Theory

B

1st finger on A

© 2024 Horsehair Music. The Magic of Music Theory Primer

A

Open A
or
4th finger on D

© 2024 Horsehair Music. The Magic of Music Theory Primer

G

3rd finger on D

© 2024 Horsehair Music. The Magic of Music Theory Primer

E

4th finger on A

© 2024 Horsehair Music. The Magic of Music Theory Primer

D

3rd finger on A

© 2024 Horsehair Music. The Magic of Music Theory Primer

C#

2nd finger on A

© 2024 Horsehair Music. The Magic of Music Theory Primer

© 2024 Horsehair Music. The Magic of Music Theory Primer

© 2024 Horsehair Music. The Magic of Music Theory Primer

© 2024 Horsehair Music. The Magic of Music Theory Primer

© 2024 Horsehair Music. The Magic of Music Theory Primer

© 2024 Horsehair Music. The Magic of Music Theory Primer

© 2024 Horsehair Music. The Magic of Music Theory Primer

© 2024 Horsehair Music. The Magic of Music Theory Primer

© 2024 Horsehair Music. The Magic of Music Theory Primer

© 2024 Horsehair Music. The Magic of Music Theory Primer

Dotted Half Note

3 beats

© 2024 Horsehair Music. The Magic of Music Theory Primer

Half Note

2 beats

© 2024 Horsehair Music. The Magic of Music Theory Primer

Quarter Note

1 beat

© 2024 Horsehair Music. The Magic of Music Theory Primer

Bass Clef
or
F Clef

© 2024 Horsehair Music. The Magic of Music Theory Primer

Treble Clef
or
G Clef

© 2024 Horsehair Music. The Magic of Music Theory Primer

Whole Note

4 beats

© 2024 Horsehair Music. The Magic of Music Theory Primer

Alto Clef
or
C Clef

© 2024 Horsehair Music. The Magic of Music Theory Primer

Up Bow

© 2024 Horsehair Music. The Magic of Music Theory Primer

Down Bow

© 2024 Horsehair Music. The Magic of Music Theory Primer

© 2024 Horsehair Music. The Magic of Music Theory Primer

p

© 2024 Horsehair Music. The Magic of Music Theory Primer

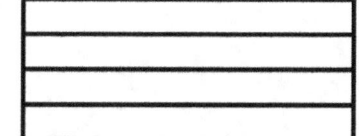

© 2024 Horsehair Music. The Magic of Music Theory Primer

© 2024 Horsehair Music. The Magic of Music Theory Primer

© 2024 Horsehair Music. The Magic of Music Theory Primer

$\dfrac{3}{4}$

© 2024 Horsehair Music. The Magic of Music Theory Primer

$\dfrac{4}{4}$

© 2024 Horsehair Music. The Magic of Music Theory Primer

$\dfrac{2}{4}$

© 2024 Horsehair Music. The Magic of Music Theory Primer

these
flashcards
belong to

_____

© 2024 Horsehair Music. The Magic of Music Theory Primer

Measure

© 2024 Horsehair Music. The Magic of Music Theory Primer

Piano

soft

© 2024 Horsehair Music. The Magic of Music Theory Primer

Forte

loud

© 2024 Horsehair Music. The Magic of Music Theory

Time Signature

3 beats in each measure; the ♩ note gets 1 beat

© 2024 Horsehair Music. The Magic of Music Theory Primer

Bar Line

© 2024 Horsehair Music. The Magic of Music Theory Primer

Double Bar Line

© 2024 Horsehair Music. The Magic of Music Theory Primer

Time Signature

2 beats in each measure; the ♩ note gets 1 beat

© 2024 Horsehair Music. The Magic of Music Theory Primer

Time Signature

4 beats in each measure; the ♩ note gets 1 beat

© 2024 Horsehair Music. The Magic of Music Theory Primer

www.ingramcontent.com/pod-product-compliance
Lightning Source LLC
Chambersburg PA
CBHW081005120626

46546CB00010B/3016

* 9 7 8 1 9 5 9 5 1 4 1 3 8 *